Whimsy Street

(Humorous Excursions from Daily Life)

Hal Reichardt

For
Shannon, Lindsay, and Conor

Acknowledgments

Sixteen of the essays in this book originally appeared in *The Oregonian*, four in *Clever Magazine*, and one in the *Portland Tribune*. My thanks to all the terrific current and former editors at those publications, including Glenn Davis, Karen Pate, Mark Wigginton, Jill Thompson, Doug Bates, Naomi Price, Pat Harrison, Sue Hobart, Lora Cuykendall, and Dianne Kochenburg.

Thanks also to my wife Shannon, who patiently read all the early drafts of these essays and let me know when the writing rang true.

Contents

Preface....... vii
Just My Luck....... 1
Every Charity Known to Man....... 3
My Spell Checker is Wising Off Again....... 7
They're Playing Our Song....... 10
Last Train to the Good Life....... 14
Shine Anyone?....... 17
Payday....... 20
Cat Fu....... 23
About Those Socks....... 27
The Horse With Fur......, 30
Feed Me....... 34
Birds Above the Bathroom....... 37
Where's My Trophy?....... 41
Beanie Baby Retirement....... 44
Signs of the Forties....... 48
No Levity....... 51
Sleeping or Not, Here I Come....... 55
Becoming Brent Musberger....... 58
What Encyclopedia?....... 61
Free Lunch Today....... 64
Popsicle Stock....... 67
Donkey Dad....... 70
Home for the Holidays....... 74
Confessions of a Stationery Junky....... 77
Reverse French....... 80
Underwear Rodeo....... 83
Be the Budda....... 87
Flu Bugs Wanted....... 90
Dads Eat the Darndest Things....... 93

Mood Music....... 96
Less Channels, More Filling....... 100
Every Dog Has Its Day....... 104
Medicine Man....... 107
Coin Collecting....... 110
Special Gift Coming....... 114
Saving Up....... 118
The Wire Eater....... 122
Kaching, Kachung....... 126
The Matinee Whale....... 130
The Final Word on Y2K....... 133
Thank You Too Much....... 136
Christmas in July....... 139
Heaven On Earth....... 142
Deeper Purple....... 145
Everything's Coming Up Whirlpool....... 148
We Are Impressed....... 151
Electricity Ghosts....... 154
My New Friends....... 158
Momzilla....... 161
State of the Onion Message....... 164
Computer Problems....... 168
Kitchen Floor As History....... 171
Letter to Oman....... 174
Musical Poetry....... 177
The Alien Handbook....... 180
Coin of the Realm....... 184
We Want The Blimp!....... 187
China Steals American Graffiti....... 190
Letter of Complaint....... 193
Two Socks, One World....... 196
Fuzzy Math....... 200

Preface

I wrote this book because I needed more enjoyment out of life. Like many people, I have a day job that's pretty great, but not that funny. So I began to write in the mornings before the sun comes up. The stories that emerged were based mostly on my own recent experiences, recast through the gentle lens of humor. With a wonderful wife, son, daughter, canary, cat, lizard, fancy rat, and guinea pig as housemates, there are plenty of experiences to draw upon. Often, it is the most irritating episodes that return to me later in my writing, transformed into whimsical essays that help me learn to laugh at myself and what Stephen Leacock termed the "timeless incongruities of the human condition." Loosely translated, that means the absurdity of it all.

I'm interested in philosophy, and wanted to use my sense of humor to develop a more positive outlook on life, the ups and downs and everything in between. But I didn't want to criticize other people or come off sounding like a cynical complainer. I was searching for something more transcendent, pieces of the thread that binds us all together on this journey. And sometimes, I felt like I found it.

My musings eventually led me to a place called *Whimsy Street*, where yesterday's problems become opportunities for re-evaluation and personal growth.

When I needed added inspiration, I consulted the past masters of whimsical humor writing, Robert Benchley and James Thurber. (I'm still waiting for answers on a few questions I sent them.)

For theories about humor and humor writing, I read several books, but found the real gem one day tucked into a dusty corner on the third floor of the library in downtown Portland. It was written by an early 20th-century Canadian author named Stephen Leacock. The book is called *Humor and Humanity*, and it's an apt title.

Because the things that really make me laugh are those that touch upon the endearing deficiencies and deep desires that make us all human. I hope that's true for you too.

Just My Luck

I've always been in love with being Irish. The sound of the pipe brings tears to my eyes, and I never refuse a Guinness Stout. Entire days pass for me in pursuit of rainbows. And I've always counted on finding a leprechaun one day sitting at the end of one of them, smiling.

As Irish as I am, I still run into problems occasionally with my luck. I wore the same green sweater for years on St. Patrick's Day before I realized that wearing a sweater in March really does makes you sweat. (I used to think it was the crowds at the pub getting me into a lather.) On the next St. Patrick's Day, I gave the sweater away to some Danny Come Lately, and watched in amazement as he won a prize for best Irish outfit.

After playing the music from Riverdance and step dancing on the bar for three hours straight wearing tight black leather pants and my new green socks, I was disappointed that nobody noticed how Irish I was. (I may never sing Danny Boy again.)

Then I tried to buy Irish soap at the store. When I found out that it wasn't green anymore, I protested to the store manager. He gave me a rain check and sent me to a sister store in Los Angeles. On the way down in the car I thought I saw a four-leaf clover forming on the highway at a big interchange, and attempted to trace the curves for good luck. They showed me an overhead photo of the clover in court and used it to prove that I was driving like a madman. The judge didn't let up when I told him I was Irish and showed him my rain check. He said I wouldn't need my own soap where I was going.

That was the day I decided to go back to the homeland in search of my roots. I wanted to find some green soap, sure, but more importantly I wanted to learn something about my Irish ancestry. On the voyage over in the ocean liner, I dreamed of singing Celtic songs with Enya, and kissing the blarney stone. (Or maybe it was the other way around.) I was going to put on a natty wool cap and walk the windswept coast of the emerald isle to listen for whispers from the past, clues to my heritage in the shape of the hills and curl of the sea.

Imagine my surprise when the rector at the church in my hometown could find no mention of the O'Reichardts in the historical records. When I started to cry, the rector did say that I looked vaguely familiar, but he wasn't about to put my name in with all the Fitzpatricks and Reillys without some proof. I broke into a jig right on the spot, and was just getting loose when I was ushered out the door. It seems that I may not be all that Irish after all.

My spirits were a little low when I left the church, but my heart leapt when I saw a glorious rainbow break through the clouds and rain. And there was a leprechaun sitting at the end of the rainbow smiling. I asked for the pot of gold, but he just tossed me a bar of green soap and said the rainbow itself was my reward. And that's Irish enough for me.

Every Charity Known to Man

T he holiday season brings out the best in me and my mailman. We work together on things to make sure that every charity known to man has a little something in their envelope to see them through the dregs of winter. The deal is that I write the checks and the mailman hauls them off to the main office to lose them. They must be getting lost because the same charities keep sending me mail asking for money, even if I just sent them a check two weeks ago. Either somebody's records are awry or my checks are getting lost. I don't care to ponder the other possibility, which is that my donations are in amounts insufficient to actually qualify as charitable contributions.

I sincerely hope this is not the case, because I can think of many other good uses for the $3 donations I regularly distribute. The problem must be with the check box on the contribution form. The form usually says something like: "Yes, I want to help fight world hunger! Enclosed is my donation." There follows a series of boxes next to some suggested contribution amounts, which normally start at $5, and move up to $30 or $40. There is also a box called "other" for the big guns who want to give more. This is the one I usually check, even though I'm not a big gun. Dastardly computers. I imagine that checking the "other" box as though one were a large contributor and sending a $3 check confuses them. However, I rest not in my mission to give a little something to all worthy causes that ask for my help.

It all started with the American Lung Association. Just when I was running out of return address stickers, they came to the rescue and sent me a whole bunch, all made out properly with my name and address. There were no strings attached. I could keep the return address stickers as a gift even if I didn't want to give a few bucks to help fight lung disease. Well, being the noble fellow that I am, I couldn't have that, so I sent them a check and used one of the return address stickers on the envelope. I liked the symmetry of that. Next came the American Heart Association and the American Cancer Society, both good causes. I was getting more American by the minute.

Word got out somehow that I liked return address stickers, and the pleas for money just kept coming. I now have amassed so many of them that I've given up the thought of ever moving from this house. It would simply be too much work to change the address on all those stickers.

Just when I thought I couldn't lick another sticker, along came a calendar, courtesy of the Foundation for Cancer Research. Wait a minute, I thought. Didn't I just give some money to Cancer? No, that was the American Society of ..., not the Foundation. These are completely separate charities, and they are not to be confused. Before long, I had a calendar collection to go along with my stickers. If anyone forgets what day it is next year, just have them give me a call. I always know what day it is, and I've got the calendars to prove it.

If I was 40 years younger, all this training with stickers and calendars would really stand me in good stead. I could enter kindergarten "ready to learn" as they say, having already memorized my name, street address, all the days of the week, and the months too!

Of course there is no going back to elementary school, so I will just have to console myself that I did get it right eventually.

As Christmas nears, the charities get excited and churn out more invitations to contribute than one Santa Claus can handle. This is also the time when I run out of stamps. If you don't get a Christmas card from me this year, it is probably because I buckled under to a postage-paid envelope that said something like: "Your stamp will help save more lives." I don't need the kind of guilt a man gets by not saving more lives, so I usually put one of my own stamps on. (My mailman thinks this is funny.)

Sometimes, when I'm furiously writing checks to keep up with all the good causes, I get into a rhythm. Now Diabetes! Now Arthritis! Now Heart Disease and Cancer! On Foundation! On Society! On Association and Prancer!

I have no idea what Prancer is going to do with a check for $3, but I'm pretty sure the letter will at least get to the North Pole. And if the mail doesn't get through, I know just whom to talk to. My mailman and I work together on things.

My Spell Checker is Wising Off Again

C omputers have done many wonderful things for our
lives, but the introduction of automated spell
checkers cannot be counted among them. There was a
time when spelling was a subject to be diligently studied
by elementary school children and casually forgotten by
college kids too absorbed in deep thoughts to bother with
details from the real world. There was a nice symmetry
to this arrangement. As a child, you studied the nuances
of our hodgepodge language and earned praise for mastering the intricacies of polysyllabic Latinate words.
Then, as a young adult, you were rewarded for forgetting
as many of these rules as possible, while stringing
together implausibly long sentences for the delight of
professors who appreciated having students with ideas
even more abstruse than their own.

The beauty of this form of torture appears to be lost on
those ingenious rascals who write our computer programs. They started out innocently enough with the
introduction of the word processor. The title for this
invention should have raised alarms in every corner of
this country, but we were all too thrilled at the chance to
throw away our white correction fluid to notice that our
efforts at using the King's English had just been equated

with the production of healthful vegetable drinks. Just put all the words in your new "processor" and stand back as they are sliced, diced, and julienned into perfection.

All right, so we missed that one. But then came the enhancements—chief among them, the spell checker. (You knew I'd get around to that.) The first spell checkers were dumb, if you will permit the accusation. These were the very programs that caused the Central Intelligence Agency and the Joint Chiefs of Staff to condemn the artificial intelligence project as a hopeless boondoggle and redirect that 10 billion dollars a year into more promising avenues such as ashtray research.

When you set off the spell checker, it would stop on any word not in its dictionary. As long as you stuck to writing plot lines for the Dick and Jane educational series, this did not pose a problem. Fancy words were, however, discouraged. The spell checker would stop two inches into your manuscript and highlight the word "the the," with the clear implication that you had misspelled this entry. Of course, we computer literates all know the difference between a stuttering keyboard and an honest attempt at modern prose, but these early spell checkers did not.

When the whiz kids got a hold of this complaint, they set about improving the spell checker program. This is known in the trades as uprevving, which sounds a might too familiar for my tastes, but we are living in a dynamic age. An uprev consists of a leap from v1.0 to v2.0 of a computer program (if you are lucky). If the uprev is of the inconsequential variety it may only merit a change from v1.0 to v1.1. Catching instances of the same word twice in a row may seem like a minor matter to those of us who are not actual programmers, but let's be generous and head straight for v2.0. No minor modifications for us!

But the world is not a simple place after all. In fact, the complexities of apparently simple matters is the secret reason why there are no old programmers. They all go gray by the age of 33 and retire to Montana to "telecommute," which is a new computer term for staying home all day.

My spell checker has now been uprevved so often (and without my consent I might add) that it has taken on an alarming degree of pseudo intelligence. In fact, if I was not absolutely certain that Sigmund Freud was dead, I would swear out a warrant that you could find him enjoying a second career writing spell checker programs. The other day I mistyped the word "beasts" in an essay about the Lions of Zimbabwe and the spell checker stopped on this entry to suggest that what I meant to say was "breasts." At the same time, an alarm went off similar to the commotion caused by hitting the slots in Las Vegas, and I was asked to remain at my cubicle while the standards police rifled through my desk looking for more evidence of repressed fantasies. I am now writing to you from Montana.

They're Playing Our Song

At an indeterminate point in the past (I can't say exactly how long ago), my wife and I entered the holy bonds of matrimony. It was a glorious, sunny day. Children played with the innocent abandon of angels. Relatives came from faraway lands bearing blenders. And they played our song.

Our song was by a band called the Pippins, which was a group formed entirely of retired admirals from the Jamaican Navy (a very select group of individuals). The Pippins couldn't sing, but man could they whistle. I think about the Pippins occasionally because they popularized one very special melody called "Stuck to You." This was "our" song, meaning the song that reminds my wife and myself of the blissful romance that culminated in our wedding day.

To understand the trouble with society today you need only examine the fact that many couples have been out getting a song without even stopping to get married. This is a dangerous practice that has been proven to lead to false memory syndrome. It is therefore not recommended. Such an affliction normally starts with the briefer sort of romance. Two people get together, one or the other smiles disarmingly, and the next thing you know they are hand in hand off getting a song. The song becomes an emblem of the young couple's affection.

The problem is that once you get a song you cannot get rid of it. Maybe a month or two goes by and the whole romance thing is on the rocks. No more smiles, no more walks on the beach, and no more linguini at Marco's. It's over, but not quite. There is still the small matter of that song to be dealt with. Just when you think you have gotten over the breakup and are ready to face the world again as a strong, independent person, some radio station will play "your song." This will bring back memories of your failed attempt at happiness. By the time you change the station, it's too late. You have already plunged into memories of better days.

You cannot get a song directly. That would be too prosaic. No. You get a song in the course of doing something else. Many couples get a song when they are out at nightclubs. This accounts for the enduring popularity of smoky tunes like "As Time Goes By," which may be the best "song" of all time, not that it did Rick and Ilsa any good. Other couples get a song in the course of close interaction in a parked car. My favorite from this category is "Stairway to Heaven," with an honorable mention to "Moby Dick" (something about that drum solo). If you listened to either song using an antique 8-track tape deck, give yourself 10 bonus points for tenacity.

Some couples have even been known to get a song while watching television. Television is notorious for getting people bad songs, but do you think that stops these people? There is no way for a man and woman to look sincere while dancing to the theme song from Charlie's Angels, and no excuse for playing the Gilligan's Island song at a wedding. Too many people know the words to that one. I have received reports on several weddings that erupted into the sort of out-of-control sing-alongs that none of us can be proud of.

While there may be no sure fire way to get a song, it is easy to tell when you've got one. There is a certain lightness in your step, a degree of satisfaction reflected in your eyes. People perceive you as being happy. Less cultured people may even comment about it. As in: "Look who got a song last night!" This type of office banter is to be ignored.

It is imperative that you enjoy your song while you can, because it may not last, even if you stay married. The other night my wife and I were in bed reading the great classics when the familiar strains of "Stuck to You" began to play on the television set. I looked up, and was horrified to see a commercial for dishwashing detergent in progress. There was no sign of the Pippins (probably off spending their royalties). Instead, I was face to face with a bunch of greasy dishes getting scrubbed into submission. That's when I said it for what may be the last time: "Honey, they're playing our song."

Last Train to the Good Life

Tax season is traditionally one of the few times of year when I'm happy about being poor. When you don't make much money, there isn't a lot to be done on the tax form. You just glide past all the categories, filling in zeros along the way. Farm income, interest, dividends, and royalties? All zeros, as long as you don't count the time that I wrote in "yes please" like it was a crossword puzzle only to have my form rejected by a computer at the IRS with no sense of humor.

I used to be able to chuckle about the problems of people who owned land and stock, or could claim a royal heritage. While I was adding up my meager refund amount, I imagined that the rich were having high tea with their tax accountants and worrying about how to adjust their gross. (It's a tight fit.)

That all changed this year when some do-gooder decided to pull me up into the middle class by giving me a few stock options. I hurried to cash them all in like a straggler trying to squeeze onto the last train to the good life before the engine runs out of steam.

When it came time to figure out my taxes, I confidently grabbed a pen and put the basketball game on the TV to keep things interesting. Everything was going fine in the first half. The Blazers were up by 20 points, and I still didn't owe a dime.

That's when I took my first lesson in high finance—no pain, no capital gain. It was just me and Schedule D. I was the good and Schedule D was the bad and the ugly.

Among the many talents of the IRS, none is more impressive than the ability to elevate fourth-grade arithmetic to a sport as difficult as professional wrestling. I took the total from line 19 and subtracted it from line 5, but the result wasn't greater than line 6, so the form put me in a double-back-breaker head twist that hurt so bad I had to hire a professional wrestler (also known as a CPA) to get me out. He looked over my form and said it was all legal, head twist included.

Wait till I tell the World Wrestling Federation about this! They will never sign The Itemizer to a long-term contract when they find out that he's has been hitting above the belt. The American public demands to know the bottom line (which is below the belt), and if these fancy pants are not going to give it to us, then I say stay out of wrestling.

Recently, the IRS was told to lay off the wrestling moves, to be kinder and gentler, and make it easier for the average person to pay up. Their response was to allow people to file their taxes electronically, which is fine, as long as you have a computer or a very powerful mind.

So I bought that tax-preparation software. When I started the program, it asked me how long I could hold my breath, and informed me that my stock options were so far underwater when I sold them that I'd probably get the bends from trying to make a premature rise to the surface.

It seems that getting rich overnight has some drawbacks that I wasn't informed about.

When I finally caught my breath, I went back to the zeros on my tax return, content to leave my options at the station and let that last train go.

Shine Anyone?

I know it's a tight labor market with the economy going so good, but when they put a shoe shine stand in the bathroom at work I was so surprised that I tipped the guy just for handing me a paper towel.

Things at my workplace have been improving ever since half of the software engineers got special offers from fast-food franchises and failed to return from lunch.

First came the newspaper, a minor entitlement that nevertheless pleases many people at a reasonable cost. One day a newspaper appeared in the lunch room, followed by a broadcast e-mail heralding the event as the first step in a program to make our company a more desirable place to work. Never mind the riot that ensued when somebody took the Living section back to their cubicle instead of leaving it in the common room.

Suddenly, soap! After years of pumping the soap dispensers in the men's room, it was immensely gratifying to finally strike soap instead of the watery solution that the dispensers used to spit up. A man with clean hands is a man to be reckoned with. I went in to my next meeting with a soaring confidence level and the cool, clean hands of a seeker of wisdom and truth.

My nose is clearing up too. I had grown accustomed to rubbing it raw with the unbleached, 50-grit, environmentally sound paper towels that my company provided. At the first sight of the new tissue dispenser attractively mounted to one side of the soap dispenser, I got all misty eyed. The tissues were blissfully white and ever so soft. My nose barely registered their presence. If it wasn't for the kindness of a few eagle-eyed coworkers, I might still have a few of those tissues hanging out of my nostrils.

It took some time to adjust to all the improvements at work, but I soon learned that taking a shine on your sneakers is not that unusual. In fact, the shine man likes me because sneakers are so easy to do. There is a lot less buffing involved, and that saves some wear and tear on the poor guy's arm.

I'm also getting used to wearing a splash of cologne. The counter around the sink in the company bathroom used to be bare, but now resembles a pagan temple. They've got a few candles going and a wide assortment of fragrances. I started out on Old Spice just to be on the safe side, but have now branched out into some of the attention-getting new scents. It's all on the honor system, so it doesn't cost much to add that certain something to your day at work. The shine man has a little dish on the counter that is already primed with a five-dollar bill, so it just seems right to throw a few quarters in there after primping up.

I bring a lot of small bills to work now so that I can take care of all the extra help we have around the building. Elevator doors open automatically most of the time, but when a solicitous fellow wearing an Edwardian hat and jacket bows ever so slightly and holds the door, a man feels compelled to throw him a buck.

I think I could do without the cubicle attendants, though. They make me nervous. And I'm not about to give that guy a buck every time he tucks me into my ergonomic office chair. I've got to save some of my small bills for the espresso cart that comes around every couple of hours.

After a few weeks of working in this pampered environment, I was out a few hundred bucks just for incidentals. And that's without once opening the little refrigerator stocked with juices and candy bars that they put in the corner of my cube.

I don't mind spiffing the people who are working hard to make my job more enjoyable. But when payday came around, I was shocked to see a deduction on my pay stub for a 14-day stay in my own cubicle. There has got to be a law against turning an office into a hotel without telling anybody.

Sure, profits are up. But when you have to sublet your cubicle to a summer intern just to make ends meet, things have gone too far. Shine anyone?

Payday

In my younger days, I was unable to find employment in the preferred industries (sleeping and high finance), so I resorted to different modes of manual labor according to the seasons. I carried golf bags in the spring and raked leaves in the fall. Both endeavors featured a payment system called handing over the money that has recently gone out of style.

Once upon a time you did the work, got the money, and spent it all in one glorious cycle after another, each punctuated by a payday.

But times change. Most people get paid electronically these days through the magic of a system called EFT, which is a code word for Especially Fast Transfer. When you sign up for this service, your boss stops handing you paychecks and starts mailing you printouts called earnings statements.

An earnings statement is a nonbinding, won't-stand-up-in-court document that provides some details about what happened to all your money while you were asleep the night before payday. Near the top of the statement is a line for gross pay. There follows an astonishing compilation of institutionalized thievery written in modern hieroglyphics. There are inscriptions like FICA, WCA, and SOC SEC. At the bottom is a number for net pay. This represents the amount of money that you get to keep during the grace period, which is roughly 24 hours.

If you don't pay all your bills and credit card debts within that time, there are computers poised to overflow your household with free loans to solve the problem. One of my neighbors almost suffocated when a backhoe pulled up and dumped 3,000 credit card offers and a few hundred home equity loan applications on him while he was out getting the morning paper the other day. That will teach you to hold onto your money. There's no profit in it, unless you are planning to build a new landfill.

The earnings statement also contains a terrific copy of a check that is watermarked so that security-minded merchants can hold it up to the light and make sure it is a real facsimile. Pay no attention to the words "this is not a check" and "non-negotiable" written on the face of the item.

Check facsimiles may look funny, but they are actually quite accurate in a perverse sort of way. They represent the illusion of money to spend without all the bother of actually spending it. Most of the spending is taken care of automatically by EFT. And, what little funds may remain after this electronic piracy is concluded are doomed to walk the plank soon enough. There are budding accountants in my household who delight in calculating back-pay for allowances missed and interest due on those spot loans that parents often require.

At least I still receive a real bill from the garbage company. I love the garbage company because they are so doggedly manual about things. The bill they send is a simple postcard noting how much money they are owed.

There is no return envelope, no postage paid, and no glossy marketing insert describing how they are going to rip me off even worse next month. If I told them I was going to pay my bill through the magic of EFT, they might just accidentally miss my house on the next pickup day.

To pay the garbage company you actually have to find a business-sized envelope and write their address on the front. I'm sure they wouldn't mind if you stuffed a bunch of 10 dollar bills in there instead of writing a check. That's my kind of company. In fact, I may just walk down to garbage company headquarters and pay that bill in person. I'll bet they still celebrate payday down there.

Cat Fu

O ur family has a young cat named Whiskers who was not wise to the ways of the world. He kept limping home with huge patches of fur gouged out of his side and a sorry look on his face. We live in a good neighborhood, so these incidents really made me angry. The problem didn't appear to be gang-related. Whiskers just couldn't fight.

He's a lover, and a young one at that; about three years old. For most of his life, Whiskers had a buddy next door named Beethoven, a friendly old fellow who was sort of a big brother to our little cat. Then the neighbors moved and took Beethoven with them. Slowly, over time, the cat neighborhood changed from a happy playground into a malevolent daily test of street smarts and survival instincts.

With no guardian angel around to protect him, Whiskers started getting roughed up. It was one indignity after another. One day he got mugged in the garage and let the other cats eat his lunch. This got to be such a recurring problem that we stopped giving him lunch money after a while. Another time he disappeared for a few days and came home covered with grease, with his hair spiked up like a teenager. That meant we had to give him a bath, never a reassuring exercise with cats (they look so skinny when they're wet).

The word on the street was that Whiskers was a pussy cat. What's a parent to do?

The answer was obvious, but it took me a while to come to the realization. It was time for Whiskers to learn the art of self defense. I thought about teaching him how to box, but I couldn't find any boxing gloves small enough to fit his paws. Then I hit upon the perfect solution. Cats are naturally agile, able to stretch and bend any way they want. Just the type of skills needed for success in the martial arts. Whiskers was going to Tibet to learn the ways of the Kung Fu masters in a monastery high up in the clouds. And I was going to be his guide.

We took the slow boat to China so that I could use the extra time to prepare my little friend for the physical and spiritual demands that lay ahead. We watched episode after episode of the old Kung Fu television show along the way, and eventually I had to concede that David Carradine was not a cat. That made Whiskers feel better about his own lack of fighting skills.

 Nevertheless, I got headbands for both of us, and insisted that we rise at dawn every day to greet the sun and practice our kicking and stretching exercises. Before long, Whiskers was asking for a simple bowl of rice at every meal. Somehow, he mastered the use of chop sticks, another good sign.

When we got to the monastery, Whiskers was brought in to meet the blind Kung Fu master. He referred to Whiskers as grasshopper, and promised spiritual enlightenment to his little student if he diligently followed the path laid out for him.

When the training began, Whiskers was an instant sensation. The monks don't see many cats, so they all paid close attention when Whiskers was learning his jumping moves. Everyone marveled at his ability to land on his feet no matter how he was tossed in the air. To test his patience and resolve, Whiskers was instructed to meditate in the courtyard for hours on end without moving a muscle. The meditation went fine until a bird flew into a nearby tree.

To this day, Whiskers still loses his concentration when there's a bird around, but the monks were so impressed with his Zen-like countenance prior to the interruption that they overlooked the unscheduled snack.

Whiskers worked diligently until one day the blind master said that he was ready to rejoin the outside world as a Kung Fu cat.

Safely home, my family watched anxiously to see how Whiskers would put his new-found skills to work. We had the first-aid kit handy just in case we had to mend up any of Whisker's old enemies. But instead of wiping up the streets with the bad cats, Whiskers surprised us all by starting a monastery in our garage. It's a new order called Cat Fu. There is something unsettling about seeing a group of cats wearing white cotton robes and headbands and kicking the air in your garage. But the neighborhood has never been more peaceful.

Cat Fu became so popular that our whole family decided to join in the fun. Now we've all got headbands and white robes. The neighbors are getting sick of hearing us play "Everybody was Kung Fu Fighting" on the tape deck in the garage, but we're giving out free chop sticks to smooth things over and that's been working well so far.

We're eating a lot more rice these days and finding a new kind of inner serenity that we never knew existed. I did a double-take when Whiskers referred to me as grasshopper, but I'm slowly adjusting to taking Kung Fu lessons from my cat. Besides, I'm learning to love again, and that makes it all worthwhile.

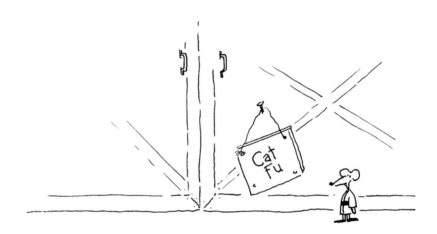

About Those Socks

I went to kindergarten resisting the notion that I should tie my shoes, and things didn't change much in the years that followed. I wasn't real keen on letting go of my free-footing ways. I did eventually knot things up in high school, but by then nobody was impressed. I lost my first girlfriend by worrying too much about my shoes and not enough about my socks.

I should have paid more attention to my socks. They have to match something, but I'm still not sure whether that something should be my shirt, my pants, my belt, or my tie. You won't get far wearing black socks on the hope that black goes with everything. I once borrowed a pair of my dad's black socks, the kind that come almost up to your knee, and bombed out of gym class after just one appearance. The gym teacher said they didn't go with my shorts, and warned me about black dye seeping into my skin.

I worried about that for a long time. White socks didn't work any better. I never liked the red and black rings around the tops of white socks. No wonder then, that this kind of sock was so plentiful that it came in convenient 12 packs. It was easy to look like a dork and hard to be cool.

So what kind of socks are cool? I think socks that you can't see must be cool. At my high school there was a certain kind of prep-style dude who would wear loafers without socks. There is an unmistakable nonchalance about this look, like a guy couldn't care less if you can see veins the size of the Hudson River sticking out of his sockless feet.

Argyle socks are cool under controlled circumstances. First, your name has to be Wee Geordie, and you must have a Scottish heritage. It helps if you smoke a briar pipe and can play the bagpipe at parties. If you can't meet those qualifications, then just take up golf. Golfers have an unusual license to wear whatever they want with impunity.

My mom started me out on argyles without the benefit of any of these qualifications, leaving me open to ridicule in the sixth grade. I wore argyles with chinos. The contrast between the colorful interwoven diamonds on my socks and the retreating white border of my ever-shrinking white pants was more than my classmates could tolerate without a few wisecracks to ease the tension.

I suffered permanent sock damage in those early years, and repressed the painful memories until my psychiatrist dredged them out of me while trying to find some way to explain my anxiety. I now wear short pants and argyles to work as part of my therapy. I have to learn to confront my argyles. I'm still on the first step, which is to go to meetings and cross my legs in a disinterested manner so that everyone can get a good look at my socks. I tend to get objections when I whip out my bagpipe, but it's all part of the program.

About Those Socks

I'm working so hard on coming to terms with my socks that I've run out of drawers in my dresser. They're all full of different kinds of socks to suit my many moods. I've got going down the tubes socks for depression, sweat socks for making believe I'm working out, and white socks with red and black rings around the top just in case I ever have to take gym class again.

But my favorite socks are the red and green ones with Santa Claus and his reindeer on them that I wear during the holidays. It's my signal to Santa that I still believe. I don't hang them by the fireplace with the other stockings because they're a little too small to hold all my dreams. I just wear them without shoes instead. And my faith has been rewarded, because somehow, some way, I always get new socks for Christmas.

The Horse With Fur

I'm normally a well-prepared parent, not given to fits of over anxiousness, but I do startle myself occasionally with my reactions to some of the perfectly harmless dangers that my children seem determined to explore.

For example, on Saturday mornings, I know ahead of time to get out a newspaper and my best Spanish hat so that I can imagine that the cartoons are wild bulls with spears stuck in their sides. I have the newspaper wave down to a fine art after several years of practice, and have passed many a cartoon under the paper with feints that would be the envy of any of the great bullfighters. My children often object to my wild gesticulations with the paper, arguing that my presence is a distraction from the main event, but I never let reality interfere with a good fantasy. (That's one of the secrets of surviving as a parent.)

When the bulls get loose (or rather, when the volume on the TV reaches an unnatural crescendo) I like to draw on my international flair once again and run down the hall as if my life depended on it. Running with the bulls is not the first choice of most parents, but I like to live optimistically. I have yet to be trampled or gored in the buttocks, and I count that as evidence of my superior parenting skills.

Running with the cartoons, however, is child's play compared to what happens when your kids reach an age where they begin to watch TV in the homes of other bull-fighters (or shall we say parents).

My daughter is now old enough to "sleep over" at her friends' houses. I say sleep over advisedly, because I know that sleeping is not the objective at these soirees. I'm sure that the main idea is to stay up all night watching movies that your parents don't approve of, and painting your nails with potions that smell like they could remove the armor from an armadillo with one easy application.

The trouble with sleepovers is that I am always at a loss as to whether I can trust the parents of my daughter's friend to worry exactly as I do. Will they make her eat her peas at dinner or will there be a Bacchanalia of pop and chips?

The dinner menu, scary as it may be, is not a bother compared to the longer-lasting impressions made by those rascals in Hollywood. I am referring, of course, to the movie selections. There seem to be very few objectionable activities that have yet to be glorified by the sleaze slingers who explore their artistic freedom to pad their wallets by selling garbage to a public only too eager to indulge the dark side of human existence.

This knowledge, along with my commitment to protect my children from all dangers, past, present, and future, is what has turned me into the Lord of Disney. Disney movies I can handle. They are often banal but always appropriate. And I find I like the music more often than not. But wander off to the action movie section at the video store, or stumble into the thrillers and chillers, and you will have me on your heels yelping like a sheep dog after strays in no time at all.

To me, a PG-13 rating means pray to God that your children skip right past 13, and R is best understood as a code word for revolting.

So, when my daughter slept over at her friend's house the other night, I was alarmed when I received a phone call requesting permission to see a movie rated PG-13. The fact that it was my daughter calling, and not the kind parents who were hosting this crime was suspicious enough on its own. But when I heard the name of the proposed movie selection, "The Horse with Fur," my imagination truly got the better of me.

The Horse with Fur? What could this mean? And if there was fur involved, why wasn't the movie rated X? I never heard of such a movie, so I called Roger Ebert straight off to get the lowdown. He never picks up when I call, so I had to resort to calling the clerk at the supermarket video counter to see what I could learn. I could hear her polling everyone at the checkout stand about the merits of this movie, but the only response she elicited was a vague recollection from someone buying canned milk that their mother saw the movie and thought it was pretty good.

Well, that's not much to go on, but it was all I had. Powerless to protest a movie I knew so little about, I said OK to the movie request and spent the rest of the evening relaxing with a few glasses of sodium bicarbonate.

When the sun rose on a new day, I brushed away my nightmares of furry horses gallivanting with underage girls and answered a knock at the door. It was my daughter, all in one piece and apparently well rested after a good night's sleep.

"How was the movie?" I inquired.

"It was sad at the beginning," she said. "But everything worked out in the end. Robert Redford played the part of The Horse Whisperer."

Feed Me

So this guy comes over to my house without an invitation, and he wants me to feed him. But first he wastes a half hour of my time telling me absolutely nothing about his important job with the government. I finally told him to see what he could find in the pantry, and he came back with his arms loaded down with Ho-Ho's.

I guess even the CIA can find the treats, not that my guest was with the CIA, because he didn't tell me exactly which branch of government he was in, but I can't rule out the CIA or the FBI. Those guys know their donuts and cakes because they're sugar cops. I mean super cops.

It's not every day that a man from the government comes over to raid your pantry. I didn't warm up to this fellow, so I snitched on him. First, I told my 9-year-old son that the treats were going down, and he came out blazing. Then I turned up the heat by telling my 13-year-old daughter. The younger one went behind this guy and got on all fours while the older one just happened to brush by and whoops, down went Mister Donut. He wasn't real happy when the cat swiped his last Ho-Ho during all the confusion.

The government doesn't appreciate outside help when they're cleaning you out. So when he asked to see my books and I showed him my super hero comics, the man went sugar high on me. I'm telling you the government is chock full of idiots. Everyone knows that super hero comics are worth a lot of money these days. But this guy started mumbling like a bad dream about the Fantastic Four being illegal immigrants, and I thought whoa, what the devil has got into this guy?

Then I figured out the game. He wanted to play "What's My Line" without Johnny Olson in attendance, which seemed like a risky idea to me, but I gave it a whirl anyway. I started off with White House sous chef, and he seemed offended by that, so I said Buddy's dogologist, and he cringed, Buddy having long since left the White House to hang out in Harlem with the cool dogs.

Then he had the gall to start asking me questions in my own home. Here's this guy high on Ho Ho's trying to find out if I've got any more treats stashed away in the garage or another secret hiding place.

I ignored his questions and kept right on with the game. "Is your job bigger than a bread box?" I inquired. This one seemed to stun him. A look of incredulity crept over his face. This was so disturbing that I dabbed a napkin with some saliva and tried to clean him up a little bit. He resisted, but I just can't play "What's My Line" when one of the contestants has chocolate all over his face.

And then a curious thing happened. It started with a shuffle and the faintest sort of heartbeat. Slowly, the mysterious man from the government started moving. Side to side he swayed, and started singing show tunes that nobody could remember the words to. "I know!" I blurted out. "You're from the Kennedy Center Awards! We must all be in for presidential pardons or something."

Well, the kids liked the sound of that, and darned if we didn't have a Ho-Ho of a hoedown right there in the front hall. Government guys. You gotta feed em.

Birds Above the Bathroom

Rents are getting intolerably high nowadays, I think we all would agree, not to mention the astronomical sums needed to actually buy a home. And yet, the high price of housing cannot excuse the family of birds who have taken up residence in the attic above my upstairs bathroom. I imagine the dad bird was flying around the neighborhood one day, spotted me out in the yard, and said: "Now here's a gentle soul! This fellow won't mind if we drill a hole in the side of his house and burrow our way into the attic." I strongly suspect the dad bird without the benefit of any real evidence, which I suppose is not the American way, but this is an essay, not a criminal trial.

I say family of birds with a hopeful tone, because I really can't be sure. I have only the benefit of the auditory sense, not being bold or stupid enough to climb a ladder out back and poke a flashlight into the area in question. They might be a pack of climbing squirrels or even a few unusual rats. They would have to be soprano rats, at that. Gather all the members of the animal kingdom together in a concert hall, and have them each take a turn at hitting a high C note. Anyone who can do it is a suspect.

No, I will stick with birds as a working hypothesis. What other creatures chirp up a chorus an hour before sunrise when a man is trying to sleep? (I have never known rats to sing in groups.) It started with a few notes of "cheep, cheep." The first time I heard this I was in the middle of a perfectly good nightmare, with my wife and children haranguing me for not doling out money in a more liberal fashion. From these small beginnings, the chirping and tweeting has recently grown to a crescendo. The mom bird must be bringing home some mighty juicy worms to warrant the degree of exultation I hear above my bathroom early each morning.

Let's just hope that birds are as selfish as us nonflying bipeds. I'm counting on the idea that this particular dad bird, the one who is camping above my bathroom in flagrant violation of the Homestead Act of 1863 (don't quote me on that) is a wily bird who would rather hand over his Visa card to a total stranger than divulge the location of his secret eyrie. This convoluted logic gives me some peace of mind that the nesting above my bathroom is under containment. It is only one bird family. And the dad bird seems to be the type of antisocial family man that I like. After all, I haven't heard any poker games breaking out up there, and there hasn't been so much as one beer bottle littered on the lawn below that side of the house. Don't even think about the birds smoking in there. There are only so many fire extinguishers to go around.

While we are at it, the remodeling work underway up there has got to stop. After the morning chorus of chirping has subsided, there is generally a lull. This respite lately has been followed closely by a pecking noise that has a character not unlike the sound of a jackhammer applied to a large block of concrete. Careful carpenters will appreciate my concern about the integrity of the sheet rock these birds are delving into.

When these efforts began, I forestalled them briefly by tapping on the wall in our adjoining bedroom. Initially, a few taps were enough to spook the birds and cause an immediate halt in the drilling, which would then resume a minute later, slowly at first, and then full throttle. Another rap of my knuckles on the wall was then all that was needed to initiate a new cycle of fear.

Birds did not evolve from dinosaurs, however, without acquiring some intelligence. Before long, I was beating both hands on the wall to no effect at all. I am only glad that these particular birds have enough decorum to keep from laughing out loud at my attempts to halt construction.

In fact, on the subject of manners, I have very little to complain about with these guests, as long as I am willing to forget that they were uninvited. They get to bed early and never steal my morning paper. And there hasn't been a single incident of their in-laws attempting to pull a motor home in there with them for a couple of weeks. Let's all be thankful for that!

So I am inclined to let the bird family stay with us, at least until the end of the season. Birds are our friends, I tell myself, and we all could do with a bit more tolerance in our lives.

Where's My Trophy?

I never get an award or a trophy, and I'm starting to get a little put out about that. It's embarrassing to sit in a room full of 50 people while a cavalcade of coworkers gets called up to the front by the big kahuna to receive trophy clocks, and then not hear your name called. Come on. If you are already buying 48 clocks, it can't cost that much more to round it off and get 50.

The company janitor would appreciate it, and so would I.

Trophies and clocks are no big deal. That's what everyone says after there is no room left in their cubicle, and their older awards start turning up at garage sales. I know about the garage sales because I briefly considered purchasing a trophy this way. After making a few inquires at the engraver's shop, I discovered that there is a bustling secondary market in trophies, plaques, and awards of all kinds.

People need recognition. If we don't give them their own trophies, we are forcing them to buy someone else's discarded award and have the engraver change the name.

But you can't buy a trophy, I told myself. You've got to earn it. That's when I decided to join the Army. It wasn't until after I was discharged four years later that I realized the Army doesn't give out trophies.

The search for recognition doesn't have a beginning, middle, and end. It is a timeless quest for validation. We come into this world without a trophy, and God help us if we leave without one. The Egyptians were so concerned about leaving this world without trophies that they built pyramids for all of the pharaoh kings and filled them with every award they could find. This made things difficult for the average Egyptian. They spent a lot of time with one hand on their forehead to shield their eyes from the rays of the sun while they searched for the trophies that kept disappearing from their bedrooms. This started a dance craze called the Egyptian that survived for thousands of years, until some American teenagers got a hold of it in the 1960s. (A few kids got the Egyptian confused with another dance called the mashed potato and ended up in the hospital.)

By the time the twentieth century rolled around, the big guns realized that they had to be more civic minded about their trophies. Instead of a pyramid with only one room, they started building skyscrapers like the Empire State Building. This way they could look at their trophy from just about any vantage point in town, but could also rent out space in it or even go inside for a cocktail. On top of all that, they could claim that they helped pull us out of the great depression. Walter Chrysler got so carried away with his skyscraper trophy that he put huge hubcaps around the edge of one of the top floors of the building. (Just let the kids on the lower east side try to steal those babies.)

When automobiles became fashionable ego boosters, trophies started to pop up on the hoods. Rolls Royce has a nice one of a gallant lady in a long flowing dress. She looks like a goddess parting the clouds out in advance of the cloud people. People in the general population began to imitate this by buying their own trophies to stick on the dashboards of their Fords and Chevrolets. Of course the trouble with this whole advance is that these trophies were not earned. You can't just pick up a trophy at the auto parts store and call it a day.

I am thinking in all earnestness of starting a society for people without trophies to protest the discrimination we all suffer. Never again do I want to have to face an employment application that includes a checkbox which says: "Have you ever won a trophy or award?" right underneath the entry for "Have you ever been arrested or convicted of a felony?"

I am also organizing a new soccer league for aging baby boomers called macro-soccer. We are all going to play soccer until we either die of heart attacks or make it to Round Table at the end of the season to be knighted by the coach, have a pizza, and receive our hard-earned trophies. This will free up a lot of space in my back yard for that swing set that the kids have been wanting. They never did like the pyramid.

Beanie Baby Retirement

I 've always had it in my mind that I would retire early from the rat race. Go off to a beach on some tropical island to ponder deep thoughts and listen to ball games on a short-wave radio. I'd have a large mailbox that would gratefully accept the incoming pension and dividend checks owed to me for a lifetime of coffee breaks and long lunches. I would never rise before the sun, and make it a point to stay up late. In short, I'd live like the slacker I've always dreamed I could be.

I'm counting on the stock market to quadruple every six months until I'm 55, but I'm not taking any other chances.

Things look pretty good right now based on my mutual fund prospectus, which features a chart with an arrow going straight up and a reassuring note that past performance is a guaranteed indicator of future success. And just in case the stock market loses its direction in life, I diversified into a massive collection of Beanie Babies, those cuddly investment animals of the earth, all nicely stuffed and tagged, with poems to boot.

My collection started with the generosity of my children. One week, Seaweed the Otter was the only Beanie Baby in the universe that could make my daughter happy. If life was going to have to go on without Seaweed, then it was going to be a miserable affair. That much was clear after the 30 or so Beanie Babies she already had retreated to a closet and cut off all communication with the outside world.

When my daughter informed me that she had to have Seaweed, and I asked what was wrong with the Beanie Babies she already had, she couldn't quite put her finger on the answer, but did nod in the direction of her closet. That's where I found the treasures of the last year, huddled together in the corner, starved for light, and chanting the name of the only one who could deliver them from their exile—Seaweed the Otter.

It was a mesmerizing performance, I must say; a bit of whimsy that had the remarkable power to pry open my wallet and dislodge about six dollars.

And so the search for Seaweed began. I will not relate in great detail the serial disappointment one endures on a Beanie Baby hunt. I will say only that I have had my limit on hand-made signs that say: "Sorry, No Beanie Babies Today." Despite their obvious importance, Beanie Babies don't have a store of their own. They seem to come through unconventional channels, and may appear at any time in an unsuspecting card shop or in the middle of a clothing store. Anything to confound the poor parent who is out searching for one of them.

When they do arise, they come in packs. It is not uncommon to finally find a store with Beanie Babies for sale and briefly dance for joy at your good fortune, only to sag in disbelief upon closer inspection when you realize that there are more than enough Spunky the Cocker Spaniel dogs to ride herd on an entire nation of sheep, but not a Seaweed in sight.

What's worse is the lines. When a rumor got around about a Beanie Baby shipment coming in at a local card shop, I pitched a tent in the parking lot so that I could get a bracing night's sleep in the asphalt jungle, and be ready to jump when the store opened. I have now lost faith in my fellow citizens for at least another week after being awakened by a honking sport utility vehicle bigger than a basketball court, whose owner thought I was taking up too many parking spaces.

It is one thing to be rudely awakened by a steroidal car, and another matter entirely when the timing is off. After I packed up my tent and made way for progress in the parking lot, I suddenly realized that it was well past noon and was forced to get in line with a group of other grown-ups determined to make it a Beanie Baby day.

I finally got my Beanie Baby, but before the week was out Seaweed the Otter was washed up on the beach along with yesterday's news. It seems that my daughter informed every aunt, uncle, and grandparent in the western hemisphere about her quest for Seaweed the Otter. True to form, the people who delight in proving that wishes do sometimes come true, bombarded our house with enough Seaweed the Otter Beanie Babies to start a colony in Santa Cruz. We had seagulls circling our house for a week, making the kind of noises that are suitable only for the shoreline, and we live 300 miles inland.

That's when I got in the game. Sensing a bargain, I purchased the entire supply of Seaweed the Otter and picked up a book on Beanie Babies to see how much they were worth. It turns out that Seaweed will only fetch six dollars on the open market (wherever that is), but there are some new Beanie Babies that are worth a lot more: legendary names like Drake the Duck, Derby the Horse, and Roary the Lion, each worth over 50 dollars now and bound to go up in price as soon as they are retired.

Retired? That caught my eye. How does a stuffed animal get off retiring after working for such a short time while the rest of us have to look cute for over 50 years? I'm just one face lift and a tummy tuck away from freedom myself, but I never figured my own Beanie Babies would beat me to the beach.

Signs of the Forties

You know you're in your 40s when you start snapping your fingers to Frank Sinatra tunes. When "Luck be a Lady" replaces "Let it Be" as a personal favorite, it's a sure sign that the ravages of the aging process have begun to addle your brain.

I never thought of myself as a big risk taker until I reached 40. Then I started going to Las Vegas on those gambler specials, wild-eyed from being up all night on the plane, and flush with the hope that I would finally hit the big one. I studied the odds for winning at craps, and dreamed of cruising the clubs with the Rat Pack. It was going to be me and Sammy, and Dean, and Frank. Maybe Joey Bishop too.

And if nothing else I was going to use my coupon for a free pull on the giant slot machine at the Riviera. But after I blew my bankroll on the nickel slots, I settled for the bonanza buffet along with the rest of the high-rollers. The muzak drifting through the air was "Let it Be," and for a moment I felt young again. Until I looked around at the other people in line and realized they were all old. Hey! I must have gotten in the wrong dream by mistake. Get me out of here!

Life's funny that way. One minute you're looking for Frank Sinatra, and the next thing you know you're at the buffet spooning out scrambled eggs and trying to decide if you want the orange juice or the grapefruit. Gotta be grapefruit. That's what the Floridians swear by, and they ought to know.

Of course, real men don't fuss about getting older. It's not cool to use moisturizer or drink grapefruit juice. A little 10W40 from the back of your sleeve and a cup of black coffee will do. At least that's what guys say publicly. In the secrecy of their own homes, men in their 40s are actually using more moisturizer than Godzilla.

You have to maintain an aura of mystery when you get older. You shouldn't wear your heart on your sleeve (or the remnants of your last oil change). And I know that aging can be more a process of gradual fulfillment than a slipping away of early expectations. Because the chips aren't all down yet.

I'm betting that my receding hair line won't pull a Magellan and circumnavigate the globe. And the odds are good that I'll be able to read the senior edition of the newspaper without that silly magnifying glass. The creak in my knee is only a strain, I'm certain. And the occasional ringing in my ear has nothing to do with hearing loss. It just means someone is talking about me (the louder the ring, the bigger the compliment).

The other day my daughter was kind enough to remark that I don't look as old as some people in their 40s. That earned her a raise in her allowance right there. When my son saw the power of flattery in action, he said I looked like I was about 10. That may seem ancient to an eight-year-old, but it was stretching it on the young side for me. Nevertheless, he got a raise too.

People over 40 can afford to be generous with allowances and optimistic about their chances in the future. Things always seem to work out if you can just remember to let it be.

No Levity

N o levity. In the halcyon days before the collapse of civilization, that was the only rule that was required. And to enforce that rule was the mission of the librarian. A hard look over the reading glasses from a good librarian was enough to stop a nuclear reaction from reaching critical mass, not to mention any hint of hilarity in that most hallowed place of learning, the public library.

The head librarian was not just an exchanger of books. She was a somber guardian of democracy, the right to know, and the quest to better oneself.

I happened to be in a building purporting to be a public library the other day, and I have grave news to report. It's not a library anymore. The first thing I noticed was a bank of computers glaring iridescently in the lobby, but that fault may be excused on the basis that being contemporary is no crime in itself. There were also books aplenty and a few people fluttering in the stacks, but they had supplanted the need for the traditional reading glasses attached to a thin chain by screwing in contact lenses of a rose colored hue.

It seems that preserving a quiet atmosphere for study and contemplation is not one of the objectives at the so-called library in the last days of the 20th century. Instead, there is a long list of library rules so bizarre that they may only be understood in the context of a civilization in rapid decline.

I know about the new rules because I recently made the mistake of trying to read a book while I was at the library. After several unsuccessful attempts to absorb an entire paragraph from "How to Make a Million without Really Trying" without interruption, I looked up from my studies and cast a withering glance at the three young girls seated across the table. They were scanning pictures from their recent trip to Hong Kong, I discovered, and giggling at all the lovely sights they had captured. Charming girls, really, in any other setting.

When they failed to wither, I disgorged an "Ahem," and addressed the group with an authoritative tone and all the gravity I could muster. "This is a library," I said.

Well, I thought I dropped the bomb, but my comment floated harmlessly over their heads like a balloon that had lost its ballast. The girls looked at me like I was a visitor from another planet and resumed their playful engagement, none the worse for the brief halt in the festivities.

Apparently invisible to my fellow library patrons, I initially thought I'd just press on and enjoy my transparency for a bit. However, I soon panicked at the thought of losing my public presence for good, and jumped into action to halt the threat.

I went right to the top, but found that there is no longer a head librarian. Instead, I was referred to a person in "reference," who referred me to the library rules previously mentioned.

Here are a few of my favorites from the list of 18 things that are not allowed: (1) Being intoxicated or behaving in a manner leading to suspicion of intoxication or drug abuse (lay off the Rimbaud); (2) Engaging in inappropriate sexual behavior such as exhibitionism, solicitation, peeping, child molestation, and entering restrooms designated for the opposite sex (keep it appropriate); (3) Engaging unwilling staff or patrons in discussions; (4) Verbally harassing, physically molesting, staring at, following around, or assaulting (in that order) patrons or staff; (5) Skating, roller blading, or skateboarding; and (6) Disturbing other patrons or staff with unpleasant body odors (can we extend this one to light rail?).

I think you get the gist. And so, newly educated, I returned to the table and informed the girls that "this is a library" really means "NO LEVITY." I then escorted myself to the door for violating rule number 3, my million dollars lost in the balance.

Sleeping or Not, Here I Come

Nature's cruelty comes in many forms: the talons of a merciless hawk, the twisting winds of a tornado, and the hairdos of the rich and famous, just to mention a few. But no form of cruelty is more insidious or destructive than insomnia. This word comes down to us from the ancient geek, and is actually a corruption of the phrase "insult me huh?" because that was what Noah Webster was saying when he rose from his bed one morning without getting a wink of sleep and decided that insomnia should be a word.

Sleep is not a complicated endeavor. A person lays down on a bed (it is to be hoped), closes their eyes, and mentally replays all of the pleasant scenes that transpired that day. That glorious drive in the minivan along the windswept coast on the way to the office. A productive day dispensing wisdom, resolving disputes, and battling corruption. Hugs and kisses from your wife and kids upon your return to the castle. Ah.

Before you know it, your breathing becomes more regular, your brain waves shift from neurotic to catatonic, and you have fallen asleep. In the morning, you leap out of bed with a smile on your face and a gleam in your eye, refreshed and ready to take on another day. So why can't anybody get to sleep at night?

I have several theories. One is that technology has simplified our lives to the point where being awake during the day simply isn't necessary any more. This has caused an alarming decrease in the need for sleeping at night. For example, these days you can put your car on automatic pilot, wolf down a breakfast burrito with one hand, and get strategic advice downloaded from your personal psychic over the cell phone without all the bother of actually watching the road. Obviously, this is a more impressive time to doze off than late at night when nobody can see us.

When we get to the office and perch in front of that ubiquitous computer screen, we are presented with many more opportunities to catch a few Zs. Terminal sleeping requires more balance than many people can muster, but with practice you can rest your hands on your keyboard like tent posts, lean back slightly, and close your eyes for 5 or 10 minutes at a stretch without anybody in the office knowing that you are asleep. To pull this off effectively, you must have your back to the cubicle entrance and disable any screen saver software you might have running.

All of this daytime napping leaves us less than well prepared to actually sleep at night.

Is there any more frustrating experience than feeling tired, getting into bed for some restful sleep, and then laying there for hours worrying about what Christmas cards you are going to pick out this year? After the first hour or so, you begin to add the additional worry about the fact that you're not getting any sleep, and that just makes it worse.

After two or three hours, you are convinced that you will be unable to do Christmas at all this year because you will have no energy due to lack of sleep. When the clock gets to 3:00 A.M., you are thinking all-nighter and remembering wistfully your younger days when such things were done for sport.

Somewhere along the line you fall asleep and set off the alarm clock.

Sleep researchers (otherwise known as insomniacs) tell us that the symptoms of insomnia only get worse as this vicious cycle repeats itself. The more mini-naps we indulge ourselves with during the day, the less we sleep at night. This causes a need for more mini naps the next day, and so on ....

Of course, this helps explain the rapid increase in the number of zombies now working during daylight hours. Their voices have a dull, mechanical tone to them. Many of them seem to take jobs answering the phones.

To listen to this message again, press 1. The next customer service operator will be available after a short nap.

Becoming Brent Musberger

Like many of life's little indignities, the need for reading glasses is a gift that just drops in one day courtesy of advancing age. Sneaks in might be a better term. One day I found myself unable to focus on the print in the morning paper as well as expected. I fought the urge to skip the want ads altogether, and strained with all my might to read the fuzzy letters. A vein bulged so far out of my neck that my children screamed like kids at a horror movie, but I finally was able to interpret the words. They said: "Wanted. Man who can read to do simple job for big bucks."

My wife kindly lowered her reading glasses at this juncture and stared at me across the breakfast table, a knowing look to be sure, and said: "Dear. I think you need reading glasses."

"Nonsense," I replied. "I just need another gallon of coffee and a bungee cord big enough to hold my neck in place. I'm not an old man."

My denials rang hollow in the kitchen that morning, and reverberated through a year of reading imaginatively. Like the nursery rhyme of old, my reading was a journey of winkin', blinkin', and nod. This is a good way to get in trouble with your fellow passengers on the bus (are you winking at me?). It is also a sure-fire way to miss your stop.

Unable to read the want ads with any efficiency, I turned to Dr. Suess for the big letters, and quickly acquired a case of rhyming disease that I still haven't shaken entirely. At one job interview, when I was asked for references, I blurted out that: "The man with the tan is a fan named Dan." That little bit of poesy earned me a trip to the front door. Nobody likes a tan anymore. A tan reeks of independent means, which is not what employers are looking for.

With my job prospects growing bleaker by the minute, I donned a disguise and walked bravely into my local pharmacy looking for a miracle in the range of 9 to 10 dollars.

I selected some sunglasses as a decoy, and shuffled up to the counter. As the pharmacist was ringing me up at the register, I quietly let it be known that I might be in the market for some reading glasses as well. He must have thought I was hard of hearing as well as half blind, because he proceeded to announce in a loud voice that the reading glasses were located in aisle five, right next to the viagra.

I looked around to make sure none of my neighbors were in line behind me, and disappeared for a few hours in aisle five. It takes time to decide whether you want to look like Benjamin Franklin or Brent Musberger. The half-glasses gave me a studious look that wasn't entirely incorrect, but they may as well have been two little neon signs that said: "I'm an old man! I'm an old man!"

The alternative was full-sized ovals of the aviator style. They encompassed my face so that I looked like an insect under a magnifying glass, and accented my irregularities to such a disagreeable degree that I wondered whether they might be part of some widespread practical joke.

For lack of a better idea, I eventually purchased the larger reading glasses and spent the next few months looking wistfully in every mirror and window I passed, hoping to catch a glimpse of the young man I once knew.

Of course, with my new reading glasses on, I can't quite see that far. But I can read the newspaper with ease. Now if I can just remember where I put that want ad.

What Encyclopedia?

I recently purchased a new multimedia encyclopedia for our home computer so that our children will have the benefit of early exposure to the digital age, and a way to look up facts about this great big world we live in. I had hoped for an entrancing experience for the kids, A wealth of marvelous sights and sounds that stimulates all their senses at once, and sparks an inner drive for learning.

Instead, I found, to my dismay, that the computerized version of the encyclopedia doesn't impress, despite the phantasmagoria of images and the smooth sounds. Part of the problem is that you can't see a multimedia encyclopedia. It's all hidden on a CD spinning away in the coffee cup holder attached to my computer.

Things unseen lack authority. When I was a child, our encyclopedia took up an entire shelf in the living room. It was proudly displayed and properly maintained with yearly updates from the publishers, a living library that grew like a snake and slithered into my imagination.

I can remember getting up early on Saturday mornings and crawling around the bookshelf, enthralled by the big leather volumes with pictures inside of mysterious places halfway around the globe. It was exhilarating to explore the world in the quiet of the morning while my parents were still asleep.

There were other books on the shelf that I didn't understand as well. Something called "Franny And Zooey," and a book of cartoons featuring a character called Pogo. But the encyclopedia I could figure out. It was all in order by the alphabet.

Like most young readers, I went for the pictures first. There were strange photographs of people from different religions and facts about the Hindus and the Buddhists. I also found pictures of the Revolutionary War. I liked the minutemen and Paul Revere. One page had a picture of the Monitor and the Merrimack, the two iron-clad ships that did battle in the Civil War. I had a hard time understanding how something so heavy could float, but the books got me thinking, wondering about the world I was in.

So the old encyclopedia worked. The new computerized version works too, but there's no romance in typing a word into the "find" dialog box. I had my own find mechanism that relied on memory. I knew just where to find the picture of the Civil War ships, and if I was off by a little, sometimes I'd see something else that caught my attention. A picture of a full eclipse of the sun or a dog covered with lava at Pompeii, frozen for all time in the spot where he was leashed when the volcano erupted and poured molten earth into the town. Neat stuff like that.

Just as my Saturday morning excursions always came to an end with my parents shuffling into the kitchen to make coffee and turn on the radio, I suppose the multimedia encyclopedias of today's world will one day give way to another imperative designed to improve our lives.

What Encyclopedia?

They can do a lot with watches these days. Maybe they will be the next encyclopedias. My friend has a message watch that he uses to get "beeped" or find out how much money he lost in the stock market in the last 10 minutes. He's never shown any interest in the religions of the far east or the mysteries of the universe, but his monthly cellular phone bill would pay for a leather-bound encyclopedia with money to spare. This guy is more plugged in and turned on electronically than anyone I'm acquainted with. He just doesn't know any neat stuff.

Free Lunch Today

Animals across the country were criticized by the Zoo Ministry again today for associating with the banned Bangu Fork society. The announcement came after Bangu Fork supporters interrupted a picnic involving zoo patrons by banging their forks on their cages demanding a free lunch. Startled zoo-goers had little choice but to hand over their sandwiches and potato salad.

When asked why they didn't just ignore the demonstrators, several people expressed sympathy for the Bangu Fork policy of free lunch for all.

"Going full bore against a cliche is tough work," said one bystander. "This nonsense about no free lunch is going down, baby, and the animals are leading the way."

In response to a groundswell of popular support, Zoo Ministry officials have stepped up their campaign against the dangers of the Bangu Fork philosophy, which combines meditation, deli meats, and side dishes in dangerous ways.

Public service commercials have flooded the networks with spots that show dazed giraffes weaving through the jungle with no apparent purpose, and monkeys on holiday using forks to dress up their long hair. The commercials all end with a voice over that says: "Don't let the zoo happen to you."

In an apparent backfire, many teenagers have started using forks for hair ornaments. And giving new meaning to the phrase "stick a fork in it," some of the kids are using them for body piercing their noses and ears.

Zoo keepers in New York tried to intimidate the animals by forcing them to read the prices for all the entrees at Tavern on the Green and the Four Seasons. But that experiment ended after several animals were caught ordering in and charging their lunches to the zoo. One board member said: "Really. You would think they would at least have the decency not to order steak. These people are animals."

According to supporters, Bangu Fork is a peaceful way to achieve spiritual salvation and avoid paying for lunch. It requires no Visa card, no corporate affiliation, and no real money.

Instead of "Om," the Bangu Fork way is to meditate while reciting the word "Yum" over and over until you reach a state of transcendental awareness that frees your conscious mind from concerns about who bought the food.

Weddings, bar mitzvahs, corporate bashes, and backyard barbecues are all frequent targets of the Bangu Fork devotees. How the animals blend into the crowd at these events is anybody's guess. A giraffe wearing a yamaka should be easy to spot. Monkeys tend to swing from the chandeliers no matter how well you dress them. And elephants leave unimistakable footprints. But the faith of the Bangu Fork disciples is so strong that they usually join the party with no resistance from their bewildered hosts.

We have met the animals and they are us.

Popsicle Stock

Ever wonder why your children know all the answers? I have. And I think I finally figured out the reason. It's plain old evolution. Your sons and daughters are supposed to be smarter than you. That's the natural order of things.

Darwin didn't spend a year on an island in the South Pacific talking to sea turtles just to make an academic point. He needed to get as far away as he could from all the wisecracks and backtalk that his children were subjecting him to back home in England. Sea turtles may not be very smart, but they are infinitely more reasonable than children when it comes to sticking to a bedtime routine.

I can't afford to spend that much time in the South Pacific, so I have developed my own strategy for dealing with the astounding intelligence of my own children. I listen patiently to their theories, and then announce that it's bedtime. If something that the kids said strikes me as forward thinking, I get right on the Web and buy stock in the company most likely to profit from the trend.

Most parents ignore the principles of evolution and work from the premise that their own experience in life is sufficient indication of their superior knowledge.

Children sense this intellectual arrogance right away and rebel. They base their rebellion on solid scientific study of the empirical evidence.

For example, being 40 years old did not prevent me from burning my arm on the muffler to my lawnmower last weekend. My children witnessed this painful incident, and dashed off to enter their observations in their scientific logs of parental behavior. But not before finding out my motivation for searing the skin around my elbow like a minute steak.

"Dad?" they inquired. "Why did you burn your arm?"

I responded as majestically as I could with my elbow and most of my arm immersed in a bucket of ice. "Kids," I said. "Sometimes your father does dumb things when he's tired. This was one of those times."

That got some pencils going. My little scientists gobbled up this remark like hungry wolves, and retired to their laboratories (I mean bedrooms) to consider this new bit of data.

I am all for the fact that children are natural scientists. But I know what they do to the subjects of their investigations. And rest assured that parents are always the subject of their primary investigations.

Consider the bugs that the children find in the yard. They all end up in coffee cans and jelly jars, with just a sprig of grass and a few air holes for comfort. They rarely last a day in confinement.

My children are not without compassion for other species, but their timing needs some work. On several occasions, I have been summoned to the bedroom window by the rousing strains of "Born free, as free as the wind blows," only to see a jar turned upside down while a dead bug and a yellow sprig of grass quietly land on the driveway.

I'm glad that I'm too big to fit in a jar, and absolutely determined not to go quietly. I knew going into parenthood that raising children was going to be an experiment in itself, an endurance test of patience, will, and fortitude. What I have come to acknowledge only lately, slowly, and by degrees, is that my own children would be smarter than I am.

I may not be the most intelligent member of the family any more, but I've been around long enough to know how to ride a winner. I noticed that eating dinner has nothing to do with the right to have a popsicle for dessert, so I'm counting on a boom in popsicle stocks to help us ride out the next market downturn. Even bears like popsicles.

Donkey Dad

This is a story about Father's Day. I hereby decree that from now on we will all refer to this holiday as Dad's Day. My apologies to the greeting card companies and department stores. Yes, a lot of neckties and 19th-hole paraphernalia will have to be relabelled. And a few thousand sappy poems will have to be rewritten, but something has got to be done.

This holiday has been getting away from its original intention, which was to honor the hard-working men who have the guts to raise children and try to teach them to make a positive difference in this crazy world. It takes no talent at all to become a father. We've got test tubes now that can handle that part. But it takes sacrifice and devotion to be a dad.

If you are confused about where you stand on this, pay closer attention to what your kids call you. If they refer to you as "father" and stand back at least 20 paces, you are either in a bad movie from the 40s or just a poor example of parenting from the 90s. If the kids call you dad and climb all over you while you are trying to have a cup of coffee and see who won the ball game that you didn't watch the night before, you are most likely a dad.

If things go as planned, Dad's Day is in for a big pro-motion. No more wallowing in the self pity that goes along with our status as a third-rate holiday. Look out Christmas and good-bye Arbor Day. We're going downtown. I want the entire village done up with banners and festoons (whatever they are). Dads of all nations are going to march right down to City Hall and pay taxes or something.

Then we'll get out our lawn chairs and park them in Pioneer Square, which will be decorated like a real dad garage. We'll have a few old cars laying around and some TVs so small that we will all have to depend on the man in front of us to know what's going on in the ball game. The bucket brigade of team TV works well in my garage, but this will be an even greater exhibition.

Whenever someone says: "He should have passed the ball" I want all the dads to say: "Yeah, he should have passed the ball."

There will be plenty of tools to play with and nothing to fix. If that sounds like your idea of heaven, then I hope to see you downtown. Rather than actually fix anything, we are all going to swap stories about how we once fixed something very similar to an overheating nuclear reactor using nothing but duct tape and a few bolts. Whoever comes up with the most outlandish story will be presented with the McGuyver Award for ingenuity, which is a bronzed Swiss army knife that you would be proud to display on the mantle above the fireplace (if that was allowed).

I'm planning to tell my story about how I fixed my son's Donkey Kid video game. My children are still in that benign state where they truly believe that there is nothing in the world that dad can't do, so I try not to let them down. When Donkey Kid went on the fritz, I took the game into the garage and got to work.

We had several electrical outages while I was working on the game due to the enormous amount of current needed to bring a dead video game back to life. I asked my assistant Dr. Franken Cat to man the controls of the voltage regulator while I went into the video game for some deep circuitry realignment. (That could have been my biggest mistake. Never trust a cat to do a doctor's job.)

When I was done, we were all out of duct tape and paper clips, but the video game was working. The software got scrambled a little more than I bargained for, but being inside a video game isn't so bad once you get used to it. My son is an expert at playing Donkey Dad (as he now refers to it) so I'm getting plenty of bananas and enjoying my amazing new jumping ability.

I'm hoping to be downloaded in time for Dad's Day, but I've been having trouble convincing my children that I deserve a day off. They seem to think that every day is Dad's Day.

Home for the Holidays

Thanksgiving never used to be a problem for me because I didn't have many family members to worry about. For years it was just me, my wife, two kids, and a cat. Just the right formula for a lazy day of football and good food. But that all changed this year when some out-of-work cartoonist with too many magic markers on his hands decided to write a book entitled "The Book of Reichardts." Among other things, the book lists the addresses and phone numbers for each of the 3,275 Reichardt households around the world. It's a long story, so I haven't quite decided whether its a comedy or a tragedy. (Sometimes it's hard to tell the difference, even in the best families.)

I pity the publisher who decided to come out with this book. It had to be an exceedingly slow year for such a long shot to even merit consideration. If the book had been titled "The Bridges of Reichardt County" or "Little House of the Reichardts," I might have given it a chance at pulling in some genre readers. Or, perhaps, if it had been called "Godzilla Returns with the Reichardts!" they could have scared a few people into buying the book.

The publishers missed their chance when they opted not to goose up the title. Even if every Reichardt household worldwide coughs up the modest fee of $145 for their own handsomely bound first-and-last edition of this one-of-a-kind book, there appears to be little danger of making the best-seller list.

"The Book of Reichardts" held me spellbound for several seconds. I was able to look up the true meaning of the Reichardt name and family crest. There was a small picture of the family crest. It shows a grown man with his hand stuck in a cookie jar. Not the sort of thing to strike terror into the hearts of one's enemies.

As for the name, there were two possibilities mentioned. One is that Reichardt means hard ruler. I know what that feels like from my days in parochial school trying to make my confirmation. A hard ruler on the knuckles always got my attention, but I'd rather not make a name for myself that way.

The other theory is that Reichardt means rich heart. I like that one better, but I could have easily adapted if my name turned out to mean rich bank account. As it stands, according to this book, there are more than 300 Reichardts in debtor's prison to this day, hundreds of years after the very idea of a debtor's prison was abolished. Not a fortune to be found in the bunch. But they have rich hearts.

You may now freely sympathize with my determination not to strike up a correspondence with any of the other 3,274 Reichardts around the world. After all these years, I don't think I could manage a Thanksgiving with the whole family.

Just as human beings have an inkling that we are not alone in the universe when we look up at the stars at night, the Reichardts always had an innate sense that there must be other Reichardts out there somewhere having Thanksgiving dinner. I just didn't want to have to pay good money for a book that told them where to land.

Confessions of a Stationery Junky

I started out on number two pencils, and the first few were free. But I never could get enough of them to satisfy my cravings. Back in elementary school, I had a desk full of number two pencils. They came in handy on those standardized tests where you had to fill in the dots to mark your answers, because filling in the dots with anything other than a number two pencil was, at the very least, bad form.

I don't recall anyone trying to get away with using a number one pencil, and I'm not so sure there is such a thing. The number one pencil is the holy grail of the stationery world. Part legend, part mystery, and always elusive, it has remained one step ahead of us.

Meanwhile, a conservative estimate puts the count of number two pencils issued since 1936 at over 1,380 for every man, woman, and child in the United States. And yet there is always a shortage when it's time for a test.

I blame this entire phenomenon on inadequate erasers. Pencils were designed backwards on the mistaken assumption that people write ten times more than they erase. That kind of confidence is impressive but misguided. Most people wear out their erasers long before they've even sharpened their pencils twice. The erasers quickly become gnarly and smudged, unappealing in the extreme. Then out comes a new pencil. And there's more where that came from, as my supplier likes to say.

If the road to addiction stopped at pencils and pens, I might have been able to rationalize my affliction as simple neurosis, a charming anomaly that lends color to an otherwise bland existence. But I couldn't stop. I had to have protractors, glue, rulers, paper clips, composition books, and yellow stickies.

Sometimes I'll go for a walk with no immediate destination in mind and find myself wandering into a stationery store as if by accident. I spend hours scanning the aisles and imagining the great things I could do if I could just find the right supplies.

My office is quite well stocked, but I have yet to launch a project that made effective use of all my assets. I don't like to start something without some assurance that I can finish it, so I am constantly in search of that one last item that will complete my collection and give me the confidence to overhaul health care, reform the international banking system, or send out at least one flyer before I'm done.

I want to make every word count, because words don't last long these days. The new composition books are called laptops, I'm told, and one is expected to write in them using a keyboard instead of pencil or pen. When you complete your labors and press save, the screen flickers and away goes a good day's work, probably to the Internet or some other ethereal realm.

I opened up one of these laptops the other day, and was shocked to see that the manufacturer didn't have the decency to print a template for Class Program inside the cover, so that a person can pencil in their expected rounds for the day, periods one through six. I was further amazed to note the lack of a table of weights and measures, a staple of any good composition book. How does a person measure the world with a notebook like this?

So I'm going back to school to learn how to use the new stationery supplies, confident that technology will transform my addiction to pencils and pens into a moot point. But I have a few pencils stashed away just in case the power goes out and I really need a fix.

Reverse French

E couter et repeter. Listen and repeat is what that means, but it sounds so much better in French, as do most phrases. French is a beautiful language, rich with history, graceful and refined. That's why I'm determined that my children suffer through conjugating verbs in French just like I did when I was in high school. The schools are always after me to be a partner in the education process, so I'm passing on the oral tradition to my kids now, while I can still remember how to pronounce a few words.

After four years of language labs in high school, where I had the expression "ecouter et repeter" emblazoned into my permanent memory banks, I still can't parlez vous, but by golly I'm sticking with the program. Unable to truly master the language, I have remained around the periphery of knowledge, boldly going where no words have gone before. This confounds some people and impresses others, depending on how well they understand desperate gestures and hopeful body language.

Most French words start out in France and come over to America hidden in a book written by some fancy pants author who wants to come off sounding like he didn't go to Sesame Street for his higher education. Other French words get their start right here in America, and make their way over to France battling fuddy duddys and high seas all the way. This kind is called reverse French. Reverse French is much harder to do than real French, but a lot more fun.

The idea is to take a phrase that makes some kind of sense in English, but sounds like it ought to be French, based on the mellifluous sound that it produces when it rolls off the tongue. Think smooth and suave. Be the beret and say "cellar door." Say it like you're Maurice Chevalier, and see if it doesn't sound French. Yes, it's reverse French.

There are many opportunities to show off your French in daily life. You can use real French if you want to be temporarily correct, or reverse French if you want to make a lasting contribution to the language. Either way, you're going to sound like a person with an accent. A person to be reckoned with.

For example, even a simple item like a hot dog takes on literary overtones when spoken in French. Chien chaud is French for hot dog. You would think that the French would reserve such a beautiful phrase for something more important than a hot dog, but that's the genius of French. Nothing is insignificant in their language. All is worthy of grand description.

Many people who didn't take French in high school seem to think that french fries originated in France, but not so. French fries were actually discovered on Coney Island in New York. This fact displeases the French people so much that they decided to punish the victim and call french fries "pomme frittes."

The literal translation for this is fried potatoes, but let's not be literal. It's so unromantic. French fries is much better; a good example of reverse French.

The French people are held in high regard in this country for many reasons, not the least of which is the Statue of Liberty, a gift that now graces the harbor in New York. They gave us Gigi and can-can girls. And existentialism. Duran Duran. Lots of neat stuff. So you might think they would be ready for some reciprocation from the people stateside.

But the French seem to be better at giving gifts than they are at receiving them. When I went over to Paris and tossed out a few of my best reverse French lines, I was expecting some applause, or at least a raised eyebrow or two. But all I got was a ticket for using illegal French and a couple of nights in the slammer.

I can now speak from experience on the matter of the language police, having been forced to read the bylaws in the original French and write on the board 500 times: "I will not make up any more reverse French words."

My children are catching on fast, however. When they found me operating a hot dog stand near the Eiffel Tower trying to earn enough money for a return trip to the states, they didn't miss a beat. They came up with a new name for the stand that our customers seem to think is delightfully continental: "Ecouter et repeter. Chomps You Lease Ay!"

Underwear Rodeo

Aging is an unkind process. Somewhere along the road we all get a stiff back and develop problems that we never anticipated, such as getting our underwear on in the morning. I wish I could blame this on the poor lighting before dawn when I rise to greet the new day. I also wish I was 19 years old again, but that doesn't help me raise my foot above my knee without pulling my back out of whack for the rest of the day.

I'm thankful that I watched all those rodeos on Wide World of Sports in my youth. This early training is all I have to fall back on now when I attempt to mount my underwear in the morning.

First I grab the side of my dresser with my right hand and wrap a rope around it a few times. Then I open my underwear drawer cautiously for fear of setting off a stampede, and delicately lead a clean pair of underwear out of the gate. I then search the arena for every cowboy's friend, the rodeo clown. When things get out of hand, the rodeo clown is the one you count on to distract the wild bull long enough for you to leap to safety. (If you don't have a real rodeo clown in the bedroom, you can use your household pet for this exercise. At our house, the cat is often pressed into service.)

Then comes the hard part. I dip my left shoulder and dangle the underwear as low to the ground as I can reach, and simultaneously raise my left foot off the ground. When the two objects get reasonably close, I attempt to lasso my foot with the underwear. Yee Ha! If I can get that first foot in, I stretch the underwear to its legal limit and spear my right foot through the other side.

This procedure does not always work on the first try. (If it was easy to put your underwear on in the morning with a stiff back, this wouldn't be a rodeo.) It takes practice to mount your underwear successfully and ride off into the sunrise. Common mistakes made by new underwear cowboys include failure to secure your right hand with a good solid rope, dipping your shoulder too low on the lasso attempt (this can leave your back permanently stuck at a 90-degree angle), and attempting to get both feet in the underwear at the same time.

The old double-foot lasso move has sent many an underwear cowboy to an early retirement. That's because the newer brands of underwear are being manufactured with fabrics that have superior elastic properties. If you try the double-foot lasso move and miss by more than an inch, it's a sure bet that you will land on the elastic band and get bucked right off your mount.

Send in the clowns? Sure, but don't expect too much. Rodeo clowns are very good at distracting wild horses, but less adept at first aid. The last time I tried the double-foot lasso move, I ended up flat on my back, and all my cat would do was circle the body and purr.

Of course, real rodeos have more than just one event. Mounting a clean pair of underwear is a good start, but you will never be a true underwear cowboy until you can toss yesterday's horse into the hamper from across the room. This can get tricky. Depending on the size of your underwear, you might have to use two hands. Then there is the little matter of boxers versus briefs, not to mention the hybrids that they are now breeding.

I have a new pair of genetically engineered briefs in my corral (I mean dresser) that has legs which extend halfway down my thighs. They feel a lot like bicycle shorts if you can get them on, real tight with a lot of stretch. Some days you want a thoroughbred horse like that, but there are times when you long for the comforting fit of an old pair of basic briefs.

One of the cardinal rules of the underwear rodeo is to know your mount, and this takes practice, so I encourage you to wear underwear every day. And there is nothing wrong with wearing a 10-gallon hat to the underwear rodeo in the morning. Just be sure not to go out front to get the paper until you have your mount firmly in place. There is no need to involve the neighbors in all of this by calling undue attention to yourself. If someone does see you, there is only one thing you can say to maintain your dignity: "I'm back in the saddle again."

Be the Budda

I have a budda that sits on my bookshelf at work. He's fat and happy, with arms outstretched to the heavens and a curious smile playing on his lips. I snagged him at a white elephant gift exchange, so I count myself lucky that the person who entered him doesn't know much about elephants. My budda is the laughing kind, and I fancy that he keeps the sky from falling with his humor.

He's not a handsome man, I'll admit. His belly is too big, and his face spills out as a lava flow of folds and tucks. But he's happy because he's at peace with himself. That much is evident.

I use the budda to hold up a row of books. I don't have a matching statue to put at the other end, but the budda handles this in a Zen sort of way, like the sound of one hand clapping. My budda is a bookend unto himself.

The books that lean against his ample waist are mostly dry technical volumes about programming and engineering. To keep things interesting, I slipped in a collection of Calvin and Hobbes cartoons, Dr. Seuss' *The Foot Book*, and an irreverent book of musings from the mind of George Carlin.

Balance is important, as the budda would tell you if he could only talk.

When I have a difficult meeting approaching, I often glance at the budda hoping for a beam of inspiration to flow into my body and lift my spirits above the rabble of discourse that characterizes most of these affairs.

Sometimes I rub his belly for good luck. And when things get really sticky, I tuck him under my arm and bring him along. The budda makes a good blind. I set him down on the table so that people have to lean around him to make eye contact with me.

"Hal, are you back there? Do you think you could join us without your doll next time?"

Doll? The budda is not a doll. To me, he's a symbol of happy adjustment to the ups and downs of life. A monument to the wisdom of acceptance. Whatever life dishes up, the budda accepts, just as he accepts himself.

But try explaining that to a gaggle of skeptical coworkers in 20 words or less and you are bound to come off sounding like a crackpot. The budda doesn't suffer 20 words or less. He's too deep for that.

So I retreated to my cubicle to grow plants and meditate. It's amazing how much work you can get done once you clear your mind of the noise that passes for communication in most offices. It was only after I retired from the meeting circuit and the e-mail wars that I truly blossomed as an employee.

It's my ongoing search for enlightenment that motivates me now. I finally realized that it doesn't matter where you are, it's what you think that counts. Now when there's a conflict at work, I just take a deep breath and smile because I know that six months from now no one will remember or care about the issue at hand. What does stay with us is our feelings about ourselves, which are profoundly affected by the way we treat other people.

In time my coworkers started to miss me at meetings, and I was asked to attend a few in the interests of receiving a paycheck. And when I came back, I was surprised by my first question, which was: "Where's the budda, Hal?"

Flu Bugs Wanted

I'm looking for a few good flu bugs. Viruses who want to test their mettle and see how tough they really are. Must be less than six feet tall and anemic with no previous boxing experience.

My ad went into the paper last weekend. I'm sure there are plenty of flu bugs in town because everyone I know is either flat on their back with a 102-degree fever, just rose from their sick bed to a round of applause for living through the worst illness of their life, or is booking passage on the S.S. Mercy in anticipation of needing a lot of extra nursing care while using up all their vacation time (now called FTO for "flexible time off").

Flexible is right. My vacation was so flexible that after writhing in pain for a few days, I ended up in a new yoga posture that even Yogi Berra doesn't know about.

Even my skin was sore. I screamed so loud while I was shaving that my next-door neighbor's burglar alarm went off in sympathy. When a new razor didn't solve the problem, I briefly considered growing a beard and renting Ice Station Zebra to watch over and over again until I turned into Howard Hughes. But I decided that I'm different. Howard Hughes was deathly afraid of germs and viruses, but I'm taking them straight on, if I can just get a few to sign up for my new outward bound program.

What I have in mind is a grueling 50-mile trek through the badlands of Nevada, carrying nothing but a canteen of orange juice (drink your fluids!) and a backpack filled with cough drops. (Viruses don't know that cough drops are the enemy, so let's just keep that our little secret.)

Things have been slow so far, but I'm working on a new brochure that I hope will pull in a few recruits.

Tired of cozying up to one person after another only to be tossed out at the end of a week, feeling unappreciated and misunderstood? Had it with dodging pain relievers and swimming through cough syrup on your way to work? Sick of watching Hollywood Squares day after day with no way to get your hands on the remote control?

Then sign up today. We're going to learn a few things about teamwork. Instead of ganging up on one person, we'll all go off in different directions and get lost in the mountains. We'll have camp fires every night, and we'll keep singing "Michael Row Your Boat Ashore" until everyone passes out or someone has a revelation.

I can't wait to see the first flu bugs repent and rush the stage in a last-ditch effort for salvation. I'm not empowered to deliver on salvation, but I can incite an infection with the best of them. I've been known to get the flu just looking at an elementary school in winter time, so I don't think whipping a crowd of flu bugs into a frenzy is going to be a problem.

When everyone is exhausted and near tears, we'll liven things up with some boxing lessons. I may not be much of a boxer, but I think I'll be able to punch out an anemic flu bug carrying a backpack full of cough drops who just marched 50 miles through the desert, sang 38 verses of "Michael Row Your Boat Ashore" after getting lost in the mountains, and just began to hallucinate about being the center square. POW! Right in the kisser. And if you want more of that, just come back around next flu season.

Dads Eat the Darndest Things

Leftovers rarely inspire people, but with the right kind of philosophy they can be very satisfying. I know, because I'm a dad, and dads get to eat everything that nobody else wants.

My own father set a formidable precedent for me in this regard. He had an old-world taste in foods that was painful to observe. I'm glad I'll never have to meet the first person who thought pickling a pig's feet and putting them in a jar for later would be a good idea. And whoever decided to stuff their leftover bait from a fishing trip in a can and call it sardines must have been a desperate man with a knack for marketing. There was also something called head cheese, which looked like baloney that got fouled up in the transporter when it was beamed from another planet into our refrigerator. I may not be much of a dairy farmer, but I know real cheese when I see it.

The closest I come to this high standard of leftovers is cold pizza. It does look funny, but many foods that seem appetizing on the first date look dreadful the next morning. Don't let this stop you. Just revitalize those leftovers in a microwave oven. (I've never figured out what a microwave really is, but I suspect it's a code word for unsupervised radiation.)

When I was practicing to be a dad, I had to eat cold leftovers or find another, more time-consuming way to heat them up. Bring back the old black skillet and a dollop of butter. There isn't a leftover on earth that can resist its spell. Everything you put in there comes out tasting good.

Why do dads get to have all the fun with leftovers? I'm not sure, but I think it has something to do with paying the bills. When you see how much money is going out the door every week for groceries, you begin to appreciate the notion of "waste not, want not."

When I was young, I never liked peas and refused to eat them. My reward for such steadfastness was to hear my parents remind me that "there are starving people in this world who would give their right arm for those peas" at least once a week. I finally stopped that refrain by stuffing a salisbury steak and some cold peas into an envelope and mailing it overseas. I got the letter returned to me for an insufficient food pyramid, but at least I tried. (There just wasn't room in there for a cherry cobbler.)

Unfortunately, when you are seven years old, your options for helping the malnourished are limited. This is where dadhood can help. The more food you waste when you're young, the more unresolved guilt you build up. When you finally become a dad, you have the rest of your life to atone for the sins of your youth by making sure that nothing goes to waste.

Don't count on your family for any help erasing your karmic debt to the starving people of the world. Help with leftovers only comes when it is not wanted. But I don't object to the children scooping me on the really good leftovers, because I know I'm slowly pulling them in the right direction. Start the kids out on little white boxes of Chinese food, and let them think they're pulling a fast one on dear old dad. Before they know it, they'll be all grown up and warming up leftovers in a black skillet, happy to have a second chance.

Mood Music

I f you don't like paying bills, read on. I recently patented an invention that helps make the bill-paying process much more enjoyable. It all started when I set out to scale the mountain of bills that accumulated over the Christmas holidays. I got a hold of some good climbing equipment, kissed my wife and kids good-bye, and set off on one of the most amazing adventures of my life.

Unfortunately, like the bear who went over the mountain, when I got to the top of the bills expecting to see a glorious sunset or meet a guru in a cave prepared to let me in on the secret of life, I was confronted instead with another mountain. (Maybe that is the secret of life.)

You know the rest of the story. I put my climbing equipment away, yelled out: "Honey, I'm home" from the den, came back to reality, and got out my checkbook.

I don't know about you, but when I write out checks to pay the many benefactors who help make our home a happy place, I mentally sound out the names as I go: PGE, GTE, and me. It's a dandy formula, but a repetitious one.

In a fit of desperation to get this alphabet soup out of my brain while I prepared the checks, I turned to the tape deck on the desk. That's when the magic happened.

We all know that many of the great inventions of all time were hit upon quite by accident. For example, floating soap was invented when someone goofed and left the lard on the stove too long. It bubbled and boiled so much that when it hardened there were little air pockets in there that made the soap float. There are a great many mothers who are thankful now for that particular invention. In my case, the mistake was that I left a Christmas tape in the tape deck too long. (I had played this particular tape several weeks earlier while I blissfully wrapped presents for my loved ones.)

This time, I turned on the tape, and the strains of Bing Crosby singing "I Wish you a Merry Christmas" filled the den with their comforting sounds. Suddenly, my mood changed from surly to benevolent as all the good feelings of the holiday season washed over me again. I went back to work with a jolly pen, and dispatched the remaining bills with good cheer.

When I was done, I sat back and reveled in the sounds of the Beach Boys singing "We Three Kings." (If you didn't know that the Beach Boys were into Christmas music, you are excused. I didn't know either until I played the new "Seasons Greetings" tape that I picked up at the gas station.)

It was at this point that I realized I had hit upon something truly revolutionary. I had just been blessed with a near-Christmas experience while tending to an everyday household chore. Why save all this fun for just once a year?

While I am awaiting approval from the Office of Patents in Washington D.C., you are free to try this yourself. Just put on your favorite Christmas music and start paying those bills. Your family may worry about you when they hear you having such a merry time of it, but they will learn to go along as soon as they realize that the Christmas music prevents you from erupting out of the den like a crazed wolf waving a Visa bill with an unexplained charge on it. "Ring a ling, ding a ling. Soon it will be Christmas day." Yes, you say to yourself, Christmas is only 340 days away. Better to be generous and broke than mean and rich.

While I haven't actually learned to look forward to paying the bills, even with the best Christmas music on, I have come to appreciate extending the Christmas spirit. As soon as my patent is approved on the Amazing Christmas-Spirit Bill Payer (also known as a tape deck), I am planning to branch out into other household chores that we generally regard with disdain, if not downright suspicion.

For example, I don't mind doing the dishes in the evening, but I never enjoyed that half hour of the day until I learned to put on my collection of James Bond theme songs before soaping up.

Now I revel in rooting out communist spy leftovers that didn't get wind of the Berlin Wall coming down. And for those really sticky jobs. I borrow my son's super-soak water gun and fire away with both barrels, all to the helpful tune of "You Only Live Twice." Dishes are no trouble at all when you do them my way: Once for real life, and once for your dreams.

Less Channels, More Filling

N obody talks about how great TV is anymore. It's been ages since I've heard anyone hum the theme song from the Jetsons ("Meet George Jetson, Jane his wife ..."), and the Flintstones now seem to be permanently stuck in Bedrock. (Wilma, I'm home for good!)

Have we all become so sophisticated that we no longer appreciate the miracle of the century? There was a time when you had to have connections to know that sliced white bread builds strong bodies 12 ways. But since the invention of TV, 9 out of 10 households are in on the secret.

The television has been my best friend for years. It tells me the truth when I've got body odor, and gives me good suggestions about the products I need to feel my best. In fact, I was the first person to actually say "get with the program," though nobody credits me for that bit of wisdom any more.

These days I find myself in the minority when I defend the virtues of television. People are more enamored with the Internet and their cell phones. There seems to be a growing preference for active participation in the human dialogue.

This is a great leap from talking back to the TV and enjoying the inexpensive feeling of superiority one gets from watching situation comedies, but I'm sticking to my system, regardless of the general tide of humanity. Over the years, television has been my faithful guide to popular culture, like a rabid hound that sniffs out the new and improved products of society so that I can join in the fun.

But lately I have sensed a change. I'm having trouble telling the difference between the commercial messages and the programs themselves, and have been embarrassed at the mall more than once when I was rebuffed for trying to buy something that doesn't actually exist.

And where is Robert Young when you really need him? I watched Father Knows Best enough times when I was a boy to get the idea about what a kid shouldn't do, but now that I'm a dad I can't always remember how to be wise and fair. Sometimes I think all I really need is a good sit-down with the ultimate dad to set me back on course. But the father who knew best is gone, replaced by the group-think of the modern family.

I noticed that the game shows are back, but they are now on at the wrong time. Game shows are for wasting time, not prime time. The whole beauty of Hollywood Squares was that it was on during the day when you were supposed to be at school. It doesn't set right to see a commercial for spray starch after dinner. And there are no substitutes for Charles Nelson Reilly and the real center square, Paul Lynde.

The best thing about the old television shows was the theme songs. They brought a ritualized sense of comfort to an uncertain world. But even that is changing. I've lived my whole life to the theme song from the Andy Griffith Show, and now I find that I am out of step. Things are going too fast for me to whistle along these days. The new comedy shows can't seem to decide what their theme songs should be and keep changing them every season, if they last long enough. I don't know what I'm whistling anymore.

I have traced our current theme song problems to a general over proliferation of channels. Once upon a time there were three alphabets (ABC, CBS, and NBC) and choosing a way to spell the tedium was literally as easy as one, two, three. Now we have surplus NASA satellite dishes formerly used for tracking radio signals from the farthest reaches of the universe parked squarely in the middle of everyone's back yard. The benefit in this system of reception is that you no longer need rabbit ears on top of your TV set.

But what good are little brothers and sisters if you can't make them take turns standing next to the television adjusting the rabbit ears and contorting their bodies like unstable statues in order to see if Sky King can save the day once again before you run out of Oreos?

Sadly, there is only so much talent to go around. So it doesn't stretch the average person's math skills to figure out that with 389 channels on 48 hours a day, there are going to be some thinly woven shows.

I am not one to disparage the average weatherman, sharing as many people do a concern about what is falling out of the sky at present, but I object to knowing the temperature in Northern Korea or the chances of rain in Guam. I will say that the 24-hour weatherman has gotten very pretty lately, and I now strongly suspect that he has become a woman. I think this helps explain the popularity of at least one channel.

As for the other 388 stations, I really can't say, because I have been unable to surf through the lot in one session without inducing self hypnosis. (Be careful when you snap your fingers around me. There's no telling what I'll do if I ever come out of this trance.)

I am sorry to say that I have become accustomed to closely following the annual sheep migrations in Australia, and now know more about the nocturnal habits of owls on the Serengheti Plain than a layman probably should. But I keep flipping the channels and scanning the stars, hoping that one of them is actually a lucky satellite that will beam down some kind of celestial inspiration to my television set, an epiphany that sets my reception back to the simple channels of a bygone era.

I don't know when my satellite is going to come in, but I still remember how to make a deal when the time comes. I'll take door number three, Monty.

Every Dog Has Its Day

S everal thousand years ago, a wise man remarked that "every dog has its day." This is the kind of aphorism that gets repeated from generation to generation, and still seems to ring true even after everyone forgets who said it in the first place. It becomes a quotation or famous saying, and ends up in a book along with other pithy observations on the human condition. It just sounds right.

I believe you would not have too much trouble finding actual dog owners to testify in favor of this assertion. I, for one, can tell you that I once had a dog who maintained that every day was his day. This was a dog that lacked any refinement, a dog with no post-graduate education at all, a dog that couldn't tell the difference between a plural and the possessive case if his next meal depended on it. And yet this dog claimed "every dog has every day" was a perfectly valid literary interpretation of this saying. "A pox on you sophists," he would often say, and that was generally enough to prompt me to open another can of that wretched food that he favored, and mull the advantages of selective interpretation.

Of course, my dog had me right in the cross hairs. I am equally guilty of reading this phrase in a way that suits my own philosophy. I like to think that wise man was talking not just about dogs, but people in general. We all have our day. The President had his day when he got elected. The Mets had their day when they won the World Series in 1969. Even my cat had his day. (Now that was really stretching things, but the current tenor of our society is one of inclusion.)

In fact, there has been a mad rush in recent years for anyone and everyone to have their day, with more than a few attempting to knead things out into multiple days, even weeks or years. We all know that there is only so much good fortune to go around. This means that any dog having more than one day is going up against some of the eternal laws of the universe, and possibly creating trouble for other dogs who have not yet had their opportunity. The pie has just so many slices, if you will.

I believe this appalling lack of courtesy can be traced back to a general speeding up of things. At one point in the 1960s, an artist named Andy Warhol noticed this phenomenon and said that "everyone gets their 15 minutes of fame." Now hold on there. What happened to my day? And if we really had to speed things up, couldn't we have been civil about it and stopped at a half-day, even an hour? No. As near as I can tell, we went straight from a full day down to 15 minutes before anyone knew what was going on. Thank heavens for the artists in our society. They are constantly piecing together the smaller signals that indicate the more important trends. If it were not for Andy Warhol, we might have been reduced to 10 minutes or so before we had a chance to have our day.

This helps explain the rash of overindulgent consumerism that we are all awash in. There are now so many dogs out trying to have their day that there is nobody left to play poker with on Friday nights. Dogs are having it their way and mastering the possibilities in ways that wise man could not have dreamed of. Puppies are being pushed by sharp-eyed marketing wonks to adopt bad spending habits before they can even get out of the shoe box.

This explosion of dog days is terrific news for the economy. The gross product (also known as dog food) has been eclipsing all known sales records. Things are going so swimmingly, in fact, that we may be able to retire the national dog in less than 200 years with only a modest increase in taxes. (He's going to love it up there in Kennelbunkport, Maine.)

Before you send up a cheer for old Sammy, the national dog, consider how we are all going to pay for his retirement. It won't cost us any money, just a minute or two of our time. That's right. A minute here and a minute there. Because once you've had your day, you are done. And a day isn't lasting as long as it used to due to the gradual speeding up of time. (This is all explained in Einstein's theory of relativity, by the way.) So don't wait. Get out there right this minute and have your day. This offer won't last long.

Medicine Man

I n the sweetness of youth, a man doesn't need a lot of medicine. There is that tincture of methiolate or iodine that the Marquis de Sade puts on your cuts and scrapes, and an occasional vitamin-fortified cupcake. But past that, many young people seem to go for years popping nothing stronger than lemon heads and red hots.

And yet, as in so many other areas of life, a balance is waiting to be paid. You can't go without real medicine for the whole ride.

Eventually, we all poop out and show up at the local supermarket to examine the over-the-counter drugs like witch doctors searching for some kind of secret spell to make us feel young again. When a teenage clerk pushing a broom finally sweeps us off the aisle at closing time, we hide our reading glasses and make a desperate grab for the box with the boldest colors and biggest promise. Inside, salvation in a bottle, or at least a one-wish genie.

This last bit of wisdom came to me in a vision one morning as I looked at the counter in my bathroom. The area around the sink that once featured miles of gleaming ceramic tile has now been taken over by an army of pills and potions, all battling to get in front and catch my eye.

I still keep a bottle of aspirin around, but these days, my aspirin looks old and gray. It often slips and falls into the sink for no apparent reason. Or has trouble getting its cap off, for heaven's sake. All the tell-tale signs of dementia. The aspirin refuses to go to the assisted-living cabinet, and constantly bumps into the new kids around the sink. Some kind of fancy pants called acetaminophen and another newcomer named ibuprofen.

Then there's the dietary supplements, or herbs for you traditionalists out there. St. John's Wort is one. I resisted it for a long time just because it has a bad name. But I've been taking it for weeks now, and haven't yelled at my turtles once in that whole time.

So I dug for the ginkgo root too. This one is supposed to give oxygen to your brain, which sounds like good science to me. And then there's echinacea, which helps your immune system fight off invaders. So far, it hasn't stopped the door-to-door salesmen from selling me more magazine subscriptions than I need, so I'm going to up the dosage and see what that does. If I can get those guys off my front porch still smiling without taking a magazine, I'll know I hit the sweet spot.

I wish it was that easy with skin. Babies have it made in this department. For the rest of us, it's a battle. You do pretty well with skin right up until two hours before your first big date, sometime in the early high school years. Then, wham! Your skin becomes an experiment in face tectonics. And just as your geology teacher predicted, the volcanoes that you get on your teenage skin slowly evolve into craters as you enter the Mesozoic Era (the 30s).

In your 40s, you begin to appreciate why the dinosaurs went extinct. It starts with a rumbling in the center of the earth (pass the bicarb). Then the craters collapse as your face starts to move. Ridges soon appear on your forehead as a new mountain range is born. Presently, your face dries out as the sun starts a new hydrologic cycle. This is the process where all the moisture in your skin gets sucked up into the clouds to reappear later as rain on your parade.

Thanks to moisturizer, you don't have to tolerate continental drift on your own face. I started out with sun screen, and worked my way up to a 50-gallon drum of petroleum jelly that I dive into head first every morning. The dermatologists all insist that you don't have to pay more for fancy moisturizers that don't work as well.

I get a lot of strange looks on the subway, but plenty of leeway too. Which is good. Because I need my oxygen.

Coin Collecting

C oins are a nuisance. They wear untimely holes in the pockets of my suits, and disturb my concentration with their constant jangling. The noise that a few nickels and dimes make when they are in the same pocket must be the revenge that the lords of finance have levied against me for not having enough paper money. It's akin to the unnerving music of wind chimes in a doorway facing west. Even as the prevailing winds activate the chimes, so does my constant lack of real money ensure than I must carry change as a mischievous reminder of my status in society.

I didn't mind so much when you could still buy something with a penny. At one time, you could put down a penny and get a full-color cartoon and a piece of pink bubble gum in return. And if you saved enough of the cartoons, you could send away for a prize. That's how I got my first telescope. By the time it finally arrived, I had already graduated from elementary school, but that didn't stop me from discovering that Mars is actually a pink planet, pulsating like a bubble, not a red planet as previously believed. (Unless my little sister stole my last piece of gum, and was interfering with the march of science again.)

These days pennies are more hindrance than help. I suspect that the Federal Reserve Bank secretly mints excess pennies just to handicap average citizens and keep them from catching their bus or getting too close to the truly rich. (Better to weigh them down than let them get wealthy.)

Unwilling to participate further in this farce, I have adopted a plan to counteract the lords of finance. At the end of each day, I take all of my loose change and put it in a jar where it can't slow me down. The next day when I go to work, my chin is set a bit higher and my cheeks have that rosy glow that accrues to the landed aristocracy from the insufferable happiness of being rich.

The whole plan goes to ruin in short order, but at least I start out on the right tack. The usual culprit is an underling of the lords of finance, a regular Joe who hands me my newspaper, and in return for a dollar bill gives me a few quarters and other miscellaneous coins.

For the rest of the day, I am a jangler through no fault of my own. When I sail into the office to get down to the business of fouling up bad guys and rooting out evil wherever it lurks, my coworkers amuse themselves with noting that the old superhero is so poor that he's got change in his pocket again.

I suffer the wry looks and whispers of superiority with good humor, and count the minutes until I can get that change deposited into my jar back in the fortress of solitude (aka my den).

Several economists have noted that collecting change in a jar is a self-defeating hobby, owing to the insidious effects of inflation. I don't see how inflation can get through a jar, but I must admit that I am not a scientist. I am more inclined to the arts, and would rather marvel at the variety in my coin collection than question its value. Through the years, I have added coins of all nations, Olympic medallions that miraculously appeared in boxes of cereal my children were eating, commemorative coinages of various ilk, and even a subway token or two.

They all get along reasonably well, but the mobs of copper pennies seem to rule the jar. It is this obvious disdain for the aristocracy of Kennedy half-dollars and vintage liberty coins that frightens me.

As I have already confessed that I am sometimes short on paper money, I see no reason to hold back now on the dirty little secret of my coin collection. I sometimes find that I must take some coins out of the jar just to meet expenses. And while it is my sole responsibility to put coins and other interesting pocket goodies into the jar, I am joined by the whole family in the antithetical enterprise of taking coins out.

School lunches are a good excuse, and there are many other defensible reasons, it appears, for someone to dump the whole jar over and pick out all the quarters when nobody but Abraham Lincoln is looking. (You'd think one look from Honest Abe would put a stop to this segregation of coins, but his influence seems to have diminished with the overexposure.)

If you will permit a brief sally into the mystic realm, I will be happy to tell you how the karma of a coin collection works. When you are in your yang, or positive flow, you will find yourself depositing coins into the jar with regularity and aplomb. Days and weeks will go by with the jar increasing coins at a rate that makes one see hope for the idea that it will one day fill to the top, and ring a bell for you somewhere in the heavens.

Unfortunately, karma has another pesky side to it, called yin. When you are in your yin, or negative flow, there is no hope for your coin collection. School lunches suddenly occur not once but twice a day, thus requiring massive withdrawals from your jar of coins. The Kennedy half-dollars are the first to go, followed closely by the Washington quarters. If the dimes begin to disappear, I light a candle and try to channel FDR to stop a new depression from taking hold.

When Abe Lincoln himself becomes a carpetbagger and hitches a ride to the bank in my briefcase, I heave a sigh of inevitability, salute the lords of finance for their otherworldly wisdom, and begin the reconstruction all over again.

Special Gift Coming

C atalog shopping isn't for everyone, I've discovered. It takes a bit of pluck, a fat wallet, and a leap of faith to plunk down $398 for a one-inch-square glossy photo of the good life. But for people who don't care to get out of bed, catalog shopping is a real lifesaver. (My mother-in-law prefers this approach.)

That's why my wife and I were both delighted and surprised at Christmas when we received a letter from a toney department store in San Francisco named Marcus Upton. The very name of this store conjures up images of a life of privilege: high cheekbones, leather shoes, and plenty of towels. The letter simply said: "A special gift has been selected for you. It will arrive shortly."

Happy day! We were especially pleased that the department store went to the extra trouble to relieve any worries we may have had about not receiving a Christmas gift from my mother-in-law by sending this letter. When all of the other gifts had been opened, and the wrapping put away, we still had the mysterious letter nestled in the holly cuttings on the mantelpiece.

What could it be, this special gift? Logic and past history left us like boarders who just discovered an empty cupboard. It wasn't going to be a huge green dress this year or another book about how to invest the money that I don't have. It was going to be something special.

The letter said so. They could just as easily have left out the superlative and said a gift was coming. But they said it was special.

If anticipation is truly half the fun, my wife and I were raising the ante with abandon. We hardly got any sleep that night as visions of special gifts danced in our heads.

The next day a man appeared at the front door with a small parcel. My wife couldn't stand the anticipation, so I was asked to open the gift. Good things come in small packages, I told myself, as I carefully ripped open the box.

But instead of an embossed Marcus Upton seal clasping neatly-folded tissue, I was confronted with a jumbled mass of what looked for all the world like butcher paper. Undaunted, I dove into the coarse brown warehouse paper, and fished out a wash cloth, an ecru wash cloth to be exact. It was from a good label, as one might expect from one of the better department stores. Still, it was just a wash cloth.

I searched the small box for any clue that would explain his gift. Was this just a sample to indicate that we were now entitled to a lifetime supply of monogrammed bath towels? No. There was no such promise in the box. Crestfallen, I dropped into the healing arms of my favorite chair, and began to mentally compose a thank-you note to the special gift giver.

"Dear mother-in-law," it began. "I am in receipt of a special gift from Marcus Upton that you so thoughtfully selected for us. It is a darling washcloth, I must admit, but I cannot fathom why you failed to send us two of these special items. If I read your card correctly, this was to be a gift for both of us. Are we to now descend on the washcloth with shears and attempt to split it evenly, or is marital strife your secret motive in sending a solitary washcloth to a happily married couple?"

No, no, that won't do, I thought.

"Dear mother-in-law," it said. "I can't stand made-up colors like ecru. Either send me a tan washcloth or send nothing at all."

Stop being petty, I scolded myself.

"Dear mother-in-law," I began again. "Thank you for the nice washcloth. I am sure I will wash my face with it many times, and you must know that each time I do I will be thinking of your generosity."

My wife thanks me now for not mailing any of these thank-you notes.

Rather than send a rude communication, we took a trip to San Francisco with our his-and-hers ecru washcloth carefully packed away in our carry-on luggage. I am sorry to admit that we just happened to be staying in a hotel on Union Square, not far from the Marcus Upton department store.

While our friends were off skiing in SunRiver, we walked past the gaily decorated storefront windows, and gazed at the fine clothing and other symbols of the good life. Tears rolled down my cheeks as I despaired of ever having toiletries and towels as fine as the well-dressed mannequins in the windows.

"Honey," I said. "Please pass the special gift. I've got something stuck in my eye."

Saving Up

Don't keep saying that, dad. So says my son, and I must admit that he has a point. He has just responded to the two millionth delivery of: "If you want a new toy, you will just have to start saving up for it." When you are five years old with an allowance of 25 cents a week, saving up enough money to buy a new Beast Wars toy might very well seem beyond reach. "Ah, but a man's reach should exceed ..." Nah, adults don't even like that one.

Let's examine this problem like the worldly citizens that we are. Child psychologists tell us that children don't truly appreciate the concept of money until roughly the age of seven, at which time they immediately demand a raise in their allowance. So, what is the point in sharing the money wisdom of the ages with a five-year-old boy?

Uh oh! Does this mean that I'm just a mean dad who doesn't want his boy to have all the same toys that the boy down the block has? That's one reasonable conclusion, and I fear that this is the type of concept that five-year-old children can understand very well. No wonder parenting is so difficult.

Then there is the additional problem of time. Here again, the root of my trouble seems to be a failure to understand the psychology of the typical five-year-old. I could show my son a wall calendar 10 times a day and still not impress upon him that next Christmas is nearly 300 days out. A child's calendar is much simpler than ours because it only has entries for Christmas, one's own birthday, Valentine's Day, Easter, and Halloween.

When we get to days, hours, and minutes, we have lost the children entirely, because they live wholly in the present. All the great religions and spiritual disciplines attempt to teach this practice of living in the moment. (This is another scrap of evidence for the idea that children are actually much more spiritually advanced than their own parents, and that aging is primarily a process of forgetting the wisdoms that we are born with.)

When you add this whole time difficulty up, you see why a child is not eager to latch onto the "saving up" hypothesis. If a Beast Wars toy costs five dollars and a child's weekly allowance is 25 cents, assuming that dad does not forget to pay it out on time (careful now!), it would take approximately five months to save up enough money to buy one. Yikes! Now I'm starting to get it. As we have just demonstrated, five months means never in the space-time continuum of a five-year-old.

Perhaps another tack would do. "What's wrong with the Beast Wars toy that you already have?"

"They have an armadillo one, and a scorpion one and ..." (He could go on all day like this if we allowed it.) The gist seems to be that the mere knowledge of additional variants in a toy family is evidence for why he needs to have them. I imagine some fiendish marketing wonk is at this very moment gleefully collecting royalties for that one statement that strikes fear into the pocketbooks of parents all across this great land of ours: "Beast Wars sold separately." You may substitute the most popular new toy for "Beast Wars" to understand the insidious global influence of this simple phrase. I have had to strap my wallet into my pants pocket with an extra belt on Saturday mornings during the running of the cartoons to keep it from abandoning me entirely.

What is it about Beast Wars that appeals to the imagination of our youth? These are plastic "action figures" of ordinary insects and small mammals. Children are curious about the natural world, and that is to be encouraged. These Beast Wars toys, however, are not faithful replications. That would be too educational. Instead, they are wicked by-products of science gone mad.

There is a human being to be found inside of all the claws and appendages of these abominations. To discover this fact, one must spend upwards of two hours snapping, bending, and folding the Beast Wars toy. If you get it right, you will eventually find some armor-clad arms and legs, and even a tiny head with an impressive mask hidden deep inside the contraption.

Upon completion of this feat, you turn to your child, who only two hours ago was begging you to snap together his toy, only to learn that he has long since gone off to another room.

Who's having fun now? Maybe I can spare five dollars for another one of these little beggars after all. (Just kidding.)

Of course, this won't do, so I begin a room-by-room search of the premises, carefully carrying the fully-snapped Beast Wars toy along with me. Upon finding my son, I gather up a bit of steam and proudly announce my success at constructing the Beast Wars toy into the desired configuration.

My son looks up from a new imaginary world on the living room floor. "Oh dad," he says. "I'm into trains now."

The Wire Eater

C ats are supposed to be mischievous and mysterious. That's their job. But wire-tapping? I thought that was the exclusive province of the FBI and the other government agencies charged with protecting us from ourselves.

We have a cat named Brownie who likes to eat phone wires. She started out on the thin wires that come on the headphones for portable CD players, and worked her way up to coaxial cable. At Christmas, when we got the tree up and all stood around for the lighting ceremony, there was a two-hour intermission when Brownie ate through the wires to the lights and sent me back to the store to get more. During the 12 days of Christmas, we went through 12 sets of lights. It wasn't until I wrapped them all in three layers of duct tape that we made it through an entire evening with the tree illuminated. Somehow, duct tape spoils the effect though. If you run short on light bulbs for your tree next year, just give me a call. I've got plenty of spares.

A wire that is only partially eaten through does strange things to the device it is attached to. It will make a table lamp flicker like a ghost, and a stereo come in and out until the back beat becomes a dying echo. These are the little clues you will find if you ever come upon a wire-eating cat.

The Wire Eater

When a wire-eating cat graduates to the thicker phone wires, there goes your privacy. First, they tap into the wire responsible for incoming calls. You will know this is true when you start getting an unusual number of calls from the pet store announcing specials on exotic birds. Then come the emergency visits from 911 every time a dog wanders into your back yard. Just try explaining about your cat and the phone line to a policeman who has visited your house five times in the same day only to find the offending dog nowhere in sight, and your cat sitting on the windowsill with an innocent look on her face, keeping watch for the next intruder.

After warming up on the smaller appliances in our home, Brownie went for the cable TV. One afternoon, I was happily watching a golf tournament when all of the sudden I got switched to the Disney channel, a premium channel that I don't normally get. At first, I figured it was some kind of promo. I called the whole family down to enjoy an old movie called The Aristocats. Brownie even sat in with us for the show. It was a nice family moment. But after the show, for some reason, The Aristocats was on again. A rare repeat, I thought, like the old Million Dollar Movie I remember from my youth, where they played the same movie every night for a week before switching. But no. This was different. The Aristocats was coming on at all hours, interrupting the evening news, and disrupting Sports Center.

And who do you think would just happen to be around every time the movie was on? You got it: Brownie the cat. I called the cable guy and pleaded with him to put in some new coax. He showed up sometime between 8 and 5 when I wasn't looking and left a bill for $9,000 for

123

1,289 on-demand movie showings. He said the cable was fine, even though it was hard-coded (a rare technical feat, I'm told).

When I presented the bill to Brownie, she scoffed at the notion of paying for her own entertainment and hinted that if I didn't like The Arsitocats, she could very easily keep chewing on the cable until she got the cartoon network dialed in for a Top Cat festival, followed by a Tom and Jerry marathon. I have fond memories of Top Cat from my youth, so I okayed the adjustment on the theory that cartoons can't cost as much as movies.

I was beginning to understand the trend toward wireless communication. I even brought in a satellite dish, but after spending a few hundred bucks on the contraption I realized that there is still a cable coming from the back of the dish to the TV. The dish gives Brownie much greater range, and we are now getting cat cartoons in several different languages.

Variety is good, but I draw the line at watching Top Cat in Chinese. Real cats don't talk like that.

Kaching, Kachung

That sound you hear when a credit card swipes through another register isn't really the sound of your fortune slipping away. I'm sure there would be more music when you go broke, some fanfare for the average person to let the neighbors know that you lived an honorable life, and filled up the bank accounts the best you could. A little recognition for a lifetime of fruitless saving and investing would be nice.

Just as there are never any birds around when you fill the feeder with seeds, there are never any credit cards in sight when you build up the bank account with hard-earned money. They swoop in later when you're not looking. So much for bird watching.

People spend most of their adult lives trying to build a wall of financial security around their families. They do it for love because most folks have been broke at one point or another and know how lousy it feels to be at the mercy of an 18-year-old supervisor at a fast-food outlet begging for an extension on an expired coupon for an apple crisp. Hunger does strange things to your pride.

Most of us eventually succeed in this quest to one degree or another, and get a few grand socked away somewhere. It's a good feeling to actually get paid interest on your money for once instead of the other way around. Kaching!

But the secret to getting rich and staying that way is to not actually spend your money. It's better to just look at it, and think about what you could easily buy right now if you were insane.

Like a riding lawn mower for your infill-development, postage-stamp-sized lawn. I could cut my mowing time by five minutes with one of those babies. But instead of actually spending the big bucks to get one, I just leaf through the ads in the Sunday paper and tell myself that I could buy one any time I want. Then I go outside and fire up my 12-year-old clunker with the 1.5-mouse power engine, and battle through knee-high weeds while the moles sit around in their lawn chairs and talk about how cheap I am.

It's no good talking back to moles, I'm afraid. They just dig more holes when they're mad. And there's no use trying to keep all your money in the bank. Not with a wife, two kids, a guinea pig, and a canary all counting on you to keep the good life going. Household pets and the people who love them have good reasons for breaking into the nest egg.

For example, our guinea pig needs a lot of extra money just to get good Timothy Hay. It has to be fresh or you're going to have problems. I found this out the hard way after our guinea pig staged a hunger strike. After a few days, we rushed him to the hospital.

The vet said: "Hey! What are you feeding this animal?"

I said: "Hay! What did you think I would feed him?"

The bill was $200 for this consultation. Now I steer clear of the day-old hay aisle at the store.

Whimsy Street

Our canary likes hemp seeds. I'm told they're perfectly legal, but at $300 an ounce I'm not so sure I'm buying that story. As long as he doesn't smoke them I guess it's all right. He likes to peck at the seeds until they explode into tiny husks that fly all over the room. At these prices they might as well be missiles targeting my bank account.

If I spare no expense when it comes to pets, imagine how I bar the door to the vault when my wife and kids are approaching. I'm just slightly more vigilant than a night watchman watching reruns of the A Team, but at least I'm awake.

I want to be there to enjoy spending my money vicariously, if not directly. It may not be easy to get excited about buying another pair of soccer shoes, but I've got quite a collection going now and they may catch on some day. I'm keeping my shoe collection in the garage, along with all the outdated squirt guns that are too small for my son to use any more.

His new one holds about 100 gallons of water and is roughly the size of a World War II bazooka. It weighs twice as much as our garbage can, so I'm not sure how he's able to lift it.

The water department had to draw down the reservoir and go to the backup wells twice last summer, and it turned out that the boys in the neighborhood were slightly mistaken when they said that water was free. Kachung.

There's a yin and yang that you have to adjust to when you're building your fortune in this world. Some of us get the money, and others spend it. It's a natural balance like night and day. Our only hope is to trust that the balance will hold, that for every loud kachung, a delightful kaching is just around the corner. I can almost hear it now.

The Matinee Whale

Fish don't work very hard. But people often give them more credit than they deserve. Take Keiko for example. Everybody loves whales, and Keiko is the poster boy for this adoration. He's been a movie star for years despite a lack of formal training. In fact, he never even moved to Hollywood. And yet, he's starred in three movies and somehow evolved into a treasured symbol in native culture and the object of more attention than the Pope.

Keiko makes us feel good about our relationship with the other species that share our planet, because we coddle him like a baby. Everybody keeps hoping that he will grow up someday, and jump over a flaming oil slick past a regatta of ships steered by evil men. That he will one day swim free in the ocean again. But Keiko never bothered to read the script. As a result, he doesn't realize that the American attention span is limited to 90 minutes of suspense, and that we expect a happy ending, not just three times, but every time we tune in.

Now, time is up, and Keiko is still swimming in circles in his protected pool. The word from Iceland is that he won't feed himself in the wild.

I know what the problem is here, and so does everyone else who has ever raised a teenager and sent them off into the world only to find them back at home fishing around in the refrigerator the first time the going gets tough. Keiko is a slacker.

Why would a whale bother to get his own fish for supper when all he has to do is swim around and look cute to be hand-fed all the food he wants? I say give Keiko a one-way ticket to San Francisco and convert his bedroom into an ocean-sized pool.

And what about those delinquent sharks that spend every summer bumming around at the beach and terrorizing people instead of hunting for other fish? When school is out, you're supposed to get a summer job. I'd much rather see a shark working the fresh fish counter at the supermarket than shooting the curl with the surfers. I realize that sharks have difficulties with all those teeth, but using someone's surfboard for a toothpick is bad manners in the extreme.

I'm not a fishologist, but my hunch is that sharks are afraid of whales, because they're so much bigger than they are, especially "killer" whales like Keiko. So let's solve both of these problems at once by putting Keiko to work as a lifeguard. Baywatch would never be the same again. We can drive him down to the shore in a big truck in the middle of the night, just like they did in Free Willy. Get him a giant chair to put on the beach and feed him all the hot dogs and soda pop he wants in return for scaring away the sharks. Our beaches would be safer, and Keiko would feel a lot better about himself.

We all have to grow up eventually and get a job doing something we're good at. Keiko may not work very hard in real life, but he looks terrific in a swim suit, and he can make a splash with the best of them. One good belly flop a day should be all that is needed to blow those sharks right out of the water. Because when you're a matinee whale, you have to keep saving the day over and over again.

The Final Word on Y2K

I don't know about you, but I was looking forward to Y2K. While I was sweating out the details of rolling over the entire millennium, my computer just sat there with a smug look on its face. There has got to be a penalty for that kind of false superiority.

I like to be prepared, so I bought the Y2K doctor software and set that off before the big event. It hummed for a while in my hard drive, and eventually found a gum wrapper underneath the desk with a two-digit date on it. The program asked me if I wanted to change the date on the gum wrapper, but I clicked on the "No" button. I didn't want my computer to have to work that hard. Now my computer thinks I'm a slob.

I wish a good scrubbing were enough to ensure my safety before Y2K hit, but I knew better. Ever since I got hooked up to the Internet, I've noticed a change. My computer seems to have acquired a mind of its own. I'm getting e-mail attachments now with pictures of my daughter's boyfriends that want to install themselves as wallpaper on my screen. Minutes from the last school volunteer meeting, and recipes for brownies. Things are so cluttered up that I can't find my spreadsheet program anymore. Now I've lost track of how long I'll have to stay in debtor's prison after the IRS finds my second set of books.

I got out on the Internet myself and tried the free e-mail site, but I didn't have the stamina to fill out the required sign-up form. I got past the name, address, and birth date all right, but I wasn't in the mood to write a 10,000-word essay describing everything I purchased on the Web in the last year. When I do write my memoirs, I don't want them to be used against me. And I already have enough commemorative plates and Elvis memorabilia.

I was secretly hoping that when the power went out on January first, my computer would crumble up in a heap and release its hold on the household. I'm tired of trying to live up to my demographics. I'd get rid of them altogether if I could just find them. They seem to work like invisible tattoos or bar codes that only computers can read.

I was labelled long ago as an early adopter, or someone who will buy all the new digital toys before anyone is sure they will actually work. I bought one of the original Macintosh computers back when they were smashing through the Orwellian nightmare of thought control better than the other machines.

The Macintosh is still sitting in the corner of my son's room holding up a few stuffed animals. I don't think it even heard about the Y2K scare. I briefly considered turning on the old Macintosh a few minutes before midnight on New Years Eve and watching it go up in flames trying to figure out what time it is.

My new computer is too smart for that, and was busy downloading canned beans, flashlights, and other emergency supplies off the Internet behind my back before Y2K. It went into survival mode. I finally figured this out when I came into the study earlier than usual one morning and found my computer wearing battle fatigues and playing war games with a few friends it met in a chat room somewhere.

I hit the deck and went for the power cord, but it was too late. I had to do 50 push ups before my computer would let me log on again and find out what else I was supposed to do that day.

I was really looking forward to regaining control of my life. The first thing I did after Y2K was ... I mean the first thing ... Well, I'll think of something eventually. I don't need a computer to tell me what my next appointment is.

Thank You Too Much

P lease and thank you are the magic words, my parents always said. So I've spent much of my life trying to please people, and thanking them for their trouble. But when I bought a new car for my wife, I got so many thank-you notes and social invitations that my mailman begged me to stop being so nice.

The first thank-you was an insipid epistle from someone high up in the car dealership. The letter noted that I was a sharp cookie for buying that new car. Did I know that the dealership rarely (less than 100 times a day) encounters an individual with my sense of style and appreciation for the finer things in life? Was I aware that with my purchase, I had gotten not just a car, but a lifetime membership in the brotherhood of man? No, I was not. This is exactly why communication is so important.

The second thank-you note was from the man who actually sold me the car. He thanked me for selecting the extended warranty and the optional rustproof undercoating on my new car chassis. He also reminded me that he would appreciate a 100 percent score on the customer satisfaction survey. He said that he would be happy to do anything he could to ensure my complete satisfaction, so I invited him over to mow my lawn and feed my son's guinea pig.

He politely declined, but our relationship wasn't over yet. Several nights later I received a phone call from the same salesman. The dealership was throwing a party, and I was invited. There would be cheese and crackers and tips for new car owners. So I cleared my schedule and penciled that right in.

When I received the third thank-you note, I started to get suspicious. Apparently, I was up for a Nobel Peace Prize and a Brookings Fellowship for showing superior leadership in the battle to revive our slowing economy. Can it be that good to pay full sticker price for a car?

Looking back, I should have known something was wrong right from the start. While my wife was sitting in the new car crying about how wonderful it was to have her dream come true before middle age makes such youthful indiscretions seem like game-show fantasies, I was sitting at a table in the middle of the showroom floor pleading with the salesman to tell me how much the damage was going to be.

What did I know about new car protocol? It seems that there are a few hundred forms to fill out before anything as gauche as money can be discussed. I finally broke under the pressure of the interrogation and blurted out a number that I thought was fair. The salesman smiled and disappeared into a back room for about a half-hour while I wiped perspiration from my forehead and endured the quizzical stares of the other dealership employees. (There he is. Can you believe that offer?)

Eventually, a man emerged from the back room and put an invoice on the table with the full sticker price on it, underlined three times with magic marker. I had just enough strength left to sign the papers. They let me go on the condition that I keep in touch, and thanked me a few times just to get warmed up.

We've been corresponding regularly ever since. Every time they send me another thank-you note, I send one back, thanking them for thanking me. I don't know how long the magic will last, but for now I'm enjoying my membership in the brotherhood of man.

Christmas in July

C hristmas comes just once a year in most parts of the world, but our neighbors seem to be trying to extend the experience. Here we are in July and they still have their Christmas lights up. Did Santa miss their house, I wonder?

I think I could tolerate looking at those lights dangling from their gables and gutters all year if they would only end the agony of anticipation and at least turn them on during the holidays.

But no. At Christmas, when I come home from work bustling with the good cheer of the holiday season, I am greeted by a darkened house next door to ours, with lights designed to look like icicles hanging forlornly in the dark. It's enough to make a man want to check every light bulb on his neighbor's house until he finds the one causing the problem. This is very difficult to do, by the way, even with a good telescope.

I'd throw another New Year's Eve party as a not-so-subtle reminder that Christmas is over, but I don't want people to think I lost my day planner too. We could have an epidemic on our hands in no time.

Maybe our neighbors lost the Christmas spirit when so many other houses in the neighborhood got the same bright idea about icicle lights last year. It has to be disappointing to see the novelty in your new lights fizzle out so fast.

I think this phenomenon is due to a disturbing lack of innovation in holiday illumination. These icicle lights were the first new kind of Christmas lights to come out in over 100 years. It's not easy to set yourself apart in that kind of environment. The trick is to let everybody else surge forward until you are the only one left with the old style. We still use those traditional red, green, and yellow bulbs. They look like they could have been on our house since 1953 (and they have). But I always take them down after New Years, and wouldn't dream of keeping them up past the Fourth of July.

I'm thinking about organizing an intervention to rescue my neighbors before they go completely over to the dark side. I'll get my whole family together to help hook up some extension cords and a generator. We'll camouflage ourselves as Santa's helpers and get to work restoring the Christmas spirit to their lights. I think a just reward for our neighbor's cavalier approach to the holidays will be to keep those lights on all year round, day and night.

Years ago, I saw a news report about a basketball player named Clifford Ray, who used to play center for the Golden State Warriors. The interviewer was at his apartment one summer and noticed that he still had his Christmas tree up. When she asked Cliff about the Christmas tree, he said he kept it up because he liked the good feelings that it generated. His tree could have used a little more water, but at least the lights were on.

At the time, I thought Clifford Ray was pushing the holiday spirit a few months too far, but now I think I see the merit in his approach. If our neighbors wonder why their Christmas lights are shining in the middle of a hot summer day, I'll just tell them that story and remind them that Santa works in mysterious ways. It's never too early to get started on your Christmas list.

Heaven On Earth

Every parent should make a pilgrimage to Disneyland. It's good insurance against the uncertainties of the afterlife. After riding on the Thunder Mountain Rail Road, I don't know if there is anything more exhilarating to be done in this world, but I'm holding out hope that heaven will be even better.

Part of the genius of Disneyland is disguising the length of the lines by winding them back around on themselves in a seemingly interminable curlicue. You start out sweltering in the hot sun and eventually get indoors, happy just to cool off. Then the nostalgic movie clips they show help you forget where you are for a while. Eventually, you move into another room, where there is more foreshadowing of the fun just around the corner, cunning visual displays, and the music of impending excitement. If you live long enough, you eventually get on the ride.

Real life is a lot like that too. We spend a lot of time just waiting for big things to happen, and often miss the small moments that constitute the majority of our existence. Waiting two hours in line for a two-minute thrill is just one example of this. Most of us conscientiously follow the prescribed program, whether that means dodging through a battalion of double-wide baby strollers in Fantasyland or putting on our ears before Mickey sails by on a magic float in the big parade.

For years, the quarterback for the winning team in the superbowl was asked on camera what he would do now, how he would top the thrill of winning the biggest sporting event in the country. The answer was always: "I'm going to Disneyland." To have so many people come up with the same exact answer is both an amazing coincidence and a testament to our devotion to the big one, that one swell ride that makes it all worthwhile.

When we queue up for the vertical drop on Splash Mountain or sit for hours in the same spot to get a better view of the parade, we seem to be hoping that one special moment will make days of disappointment disappear like our own shadows when the sun finally reaches its zenith directly overhead.

But Disney has the real secret to enjoying life. The trick is to enjoy the line. It's often shorter than you think. And if you focus on the line itself, you miss some of the fun. It's better to talk to the people close to you, be the breeze, and soak up the sun. Watch as throngs of people scurry by in a frenzy to find what you've already got, a chance to stop the world and just be a mousketeer for a while.

There is nothing wrong with big events. Graduating from school, getting married, and having a child are all exceptional experiences. The trouble is that there just aren't enough of these to fill up a whole life.

And not all of the big thrills turn out like you expect. I waited for hours to get on "It's a Small World" only to be embarrassed when I discovered I was the only person on the boat who couldn't remember the words to that classic song. For one terrifying moment the beautiful visual displays seemed to morph into cheesy cardboard cutouts of the different children of the world, all chiding me for my lack of harmony.

But oh, the air conditioning. By the time we made it around the world, I was singing too. Now my family wishes I never did learn all the words, because I can't seem to stop.

Deeper Purple

T he benefits of fogeyism are few, but getting older isn't all bad. One of the fun things is a good music revival. There is a curious musical phenomenon that happens with people called branding. This is the process where whatever music happened to be playing on the radio on your 22nd birthday gets permanently burned into your read-only memory like a brand seared into a side of beef while it's still on the hoof.

At 22, the world is still an oyster that hasn't cracked all the way open yet. Things smell a little funny, but there's a lot of goo yet to be revealed. While in this transitional state, we turn to music for comfort. Music somehow reconciles the surging hormones and low wages with our great expectations for the future.

I survived my branding with good cheer, and actually enjoyed the ritual. What I didn't realize at the time was the cost of higher consciousness. For example, Deep Purple was one of the bands getting a lot of air play when I turned 22. They were early explorers in the land of heavy metal, along with other groups like Led Zeppelin. Many people can name at least one of their songs, and I'm betting that "Smoke on the Water" would win a contest of this kind. If you don't remember all the words, just play along with me for a moment here: "Smoke on the water, a fire in the sky." (It's better with the bass.)

Whimsy Street

The down payment for my personal enlightenment amounted to the cost of an 8-track tape and a vinyl record album. I had to have the tape to play in my car and the record to play in my bedroom.

First thing in the morning it was Smoke on the Waterbed, and on the way to work it was Highway Star. When people hear that song blaring from a powder-blue, 1962 Riviera with a 4-barrel 445, and see a young man at the wheel, jerking his head back and forth with the beat at a stop light, they give you a wide berth. So I always got to work in one piece somehow.

My parents were not big Deep Purple fans, but they seemed to understand music branding well enough. Here we were in the fabulous 70s, and all they would listen to on the radio was the music of the 30s, 40s, and 50s. If you want to understand the generation gap, just picture Frank Sinatra duking it out with Deep Purple.

I avoided such confrontations by going deaf. I had the music on so loud in my upstairs bedroom that I couldn't hear my parents yelling up the stairs to turn it down. So, during meals and other family times, it was "one for the road" with Frank, and the rest of the time it was my music.

I had a flashback recently at the music store. With my 8-track tape long since taking up space in a landfill somewhere, and my vinyl record all but forgotten, I chanced upon a Deep Purple CD called Machine Head with all my favorite songs. There were the heavy metal gurus of my youth on the cover, looking just like they did 30 years ago, with long hair and everything.

So I bought Machine Head for the third time, and it all came back to me: the smoke, the water, and the fire in the sky. It would have been my fourth copy, but I missed the casette version due to a long period of disenlightenment I sunk into about the time that I realized two kids and a mortgage were going to mean getting a job that lasts longer than six months.

But I'm back now, and I'm looking more like Frank Sinatra every day. The kids don't quite understand air guitar yet, but they seem to appreciate the effort.

Everything's Coming Up Whirlpool

There's one cycle to the life of a homeowner that you only get to see every 10 years or so. It's akin to celestial events like comets and eclipses that come around now and then to amaze the less-informed natives, but it costs a lot more.

I'm talking about appliances. If you're like me, you probably purchased a washer and dryer when you moved into your home. I can remember the pride I felt at finally having a washer and dryer that don't require quarters to operate. Suddenly, we could wash, rinse, and spin to our heart's content without subjecting our undergarments to public scrutiny.

My son refers to our laundry room as "the factory." When judged in terms of the constant stream of jarring noises that emanate from that area of the house, I believe this is an appropriate designation. In a family with two children, there never seems to be a moment when a "load" isn't being put through the factory.

Then there are the mystery loads that go through when you are trying to sleep. Thuds and bumps and rattles in the night. I like to blame all unaccounted-for noises on the laundry room because it's simpler that way. I don't want to think too much about the possibility of ghosts or intruders in the dark.

Then one day comes a flood that would be in the bible if updates were allowed. Water streams out of the laundry room in a nonstop torrent, and you know what comes next. Time to call the appliance repair company.

Eventually, a man pulls up in a work truck and comes inside to the factory. After a time that seems like an eternity but is probably more like one minute, he says: "Oh, yeah. Here's your problem. This washing machine is 10 years old. What are you trying to pull around here? Didn't you see The Lion King? Don't you know anything about the cycle of life?"

"I think you mean circle of life," I said.

"Whatever," comes the response.

Later in the day, a new washing machine appears and takes its rightful place in the factory, next to the dryer. And that is when the true meaning of synchronicity becomes apparent. You can set a stopwatch on this if you don't believe me, but I guarantee you the dryer will start misbehaving within a week. So, after the flood comes the fire in the overheated dryer. There is nothing quite like the smell of a few mismatched socks roasting in a dryer with a bad thermostat. (I'm told matched socks smell much sweeter when they burn, but I'll have to wait another 10 years to try that one, assuming I can match my socks by then.)

Again comes the service man, and again the look of astonishment that any homeowner would have the gall to put a brand new washing machine right next to a 10-year-old dryer.

Two down and one home equity loan to go. Because things don't just happen in twos. They come in threes. For the next week, while the rest of the family was celebrating the arrival of our new washer and dryer, I was on a vigil, anxiously waiting for something else to break.

I didn't have to wait long, because right around bedtime a jarring noise ripped through the night. It was unlike anything I'd ever heard before. I rounded up the usual suspects, but the burglar alarm and smoke detector both had solid alibis, and the cat was fast asleep in the garage.

This time there was no man to call, nowhere to turn except to my wife, who was calmly sleeping through the whole crisis. The third shoe had dropped, and I was the only one who seemed to care.

She just rolled over and said "It's the new dryer, honey. Isn't it great? It lets you know when the load is done."

We Are Impressed

D ear Mr. Reichardt:
We are impressed with the way you've handled your investments during the recent market downturn. You generated so many commissions for us that we all moved to Bermuda. When you covered your shorts, we put on our swim trunks too. When you were hoisted on your own petard, we hoisted a few drinks as well. We now have several cocktails competing for "best petard."

Something in the way you moved made the markets sputter. You had the reaction time of a fighter pilot. When there was even so much as a whiff of a cloud on the horizon, you pulled the trigger. You may be the only investor in history to buy and sell the same stock 100 times in one day based on weather reports from around the world. Although it has now been shown that rain doesn't make everything grow, we applaud you for an inspired hypothesis.

Raw fundamentals never stopped you from great leaps of imagination, and we are grateful for that. You thrilled to the revelation that revenues were almost as good as earnings. When a company slowed the rate that it lost money, you spotted the trend. When representatives from the old economy came knocking at your door, you tore up your bills and kicked them out for being hopelessly outdated. Now, you're getting by just fine without heat and electricity!

May I say sir, that you are an inspiration to the natives here on the island. We have been regaling them with tales of your high-growth strategies for the new global economy, and they are proud to lend you a little seed money for your next venture. Better act fast, because we're cutting back on tips. (I understand that the mango seeds grow into particularly handsome plants.)

Those pork belly futures that you purchased have finally come in. You may take delivery any time now, but watch that cholesterol. I'm afraid that you will have to commission a fleet of trucks to haul away your investment. Look out for those pesky local ordinances about farming in the metropolitan area. Your immediate attention to this matter is appreciated, as there is no way we can keep 1,000 pigs busy at our offices. (This has been tried before and resulted in heavy layoffs.) If you're thinking Bermuda would make a nice home for the little squealers, I'm sorry to inform you that pigs without margin accounts are not welcome here on the island.

You are a new breed of visionary, my friend. Wily and fast afinger, you used our online trading service to dodge every worthwhile investment with a contrarian streak never before seen by this firm. Somehow, you managed to parlay one bad stock pick into an ever-changing portfolio of companies with innovative ideas and dubious products. Remember, they laughed at Columbus too before he fell off the end of the earth on his way to India.

We Are Impressed

Up next, may we suggest a passbook savings account? Your balance has unfortunately dipped below our minimum requirements.

Yours truly,
Bolingsbroke, Fierce, Penny, and Cride

Electricity Ghosts

I'm always prepared for the unexpected. I've got plenty of spam, tons of canned beans, and a radio permanently tuned to the emergency broadcasting system (it just hums when you turn it on, but that's only because it's peace time). I like to keep things in good working order like that, ready for anything.

So last Friday when the overhead light in the study didn't work, I thought, no problem. I'll just change the light bulb. I've got plenty of spares. But I tried a new bulb, and that one didn't work either.

I got out a stool and went eye to eye with the light fixture. I stared at it for a long time, but didn't get any response, so I decided to take it apart. Whoa, I thought. Don't forget your basics about electricity. You have to shut off the power before you work on a light fixture.

So I went down to the garage and got out my flashlight with the dead batteries. Then I squinted at the doodles on the diagram next to my circuit breakers. I ran out of matches before I could decipher the code, so I decided to stay on the safe side and shut everything off.

If you want to find out what your whole family is doing from one central location, just turn off the power. You get a cascading effect as the change ripples through the house. "The TV's out," my son screams, "The dryer's not tumbling," says my wife, and "My music won't play," from my daughter.

OK. All present and accounted for. I got the whole family together and waved my dead flashlight at them like a priest anointing the faithful. "Listen up," I said. "I'm going to teach you a little something about safety and preparedness. When a light bulb goes out, what's the first thing you do?"

"Tell dad," says my son.

That wasn't the answer I was looking for, but I didn't want to dispute my importance to the household. "Well, yes," I said. "And if dad's not around, you turn off the circuit breakers. You don't want to get electrocuted."

My son thought about that for a while and then said: "I think it was ghosts. They get mad and turn off the lights sometimes."

Well sure, ghosts. I didn't want to destroy my son's world view with too much emphasis on the scientific method, so I patted him on the head and nodded as though ghosts were a definite possibility.

Then I showed everyone the real evidence. "You see this can light?" I said, pointing to the offending fixture. "Feel how hot that is."

One by one, everyone in the family got up on the chair and touched the edge of the light fixture. There was general agreement that it was warm.

"There. That proves that what we've got here is a short circuit. A wire got frayed or something. Do you know how dangerous that is?" I gestured so emphatically at this point that the top came off my flashlight and the two dead batteries shot into the couch like torpedoes. Luckily, I missed the cat, who was sleeping on the job again.

"Does that mean I can't play my music?" my daughter asked.

"I'm afraid so honey," I said. "But at least we're all safe because your dad is smart enough to cut off the power when there's a short circuit in the house."

A knock on the front door broke everyone's concentration, so I wrapped up the safety lecture, and we all went downstairs. It was my neighbor, Bob.

"I saw the lights go out in your house, so I thought I'd come over to see if I could help," said Bob. I quickly explained to Bob about the short circuit and how I saved the family. He seemed impressed.

We went upstairs and Bob pulled the light fixture right out of the ceiling to check the wires. I made a note of that little technique, and then looked at the wires causing the short.

"These look all right to me," said Bob. "Why don't you flip the circuit breaker back on and we'll watch it." Everyone gathered around in nervous anticipation as if we were lighting the Christmas tree in Rockefeller Center. "Power on," I yelled from the basement, as I flipped the switch.

Screams of excitement erupted from the study, and I dashed up the stairs to see for myself what was happening. The light was on! "But it didn't work when I turned it on, and I tried two different bulbs," I said.

"Oh, these things happen," said Bob. "Probably just a ghost."

My son looked at me like a cat who just ate a canary. All I could do was nod and mumble something about safety first. Then I went to the store to get some new batteries for the flashlight. I never want to be unprepared like that again.

My New Friends

And how are you this evening, Mr. Ryechard? Thus starts another intimate conversation with one of my new friends. Just when I thought I was beginning to lose some of my personal appeal, I was contacted by some new people who really seem to care about me.

When I was young, my father told me that I would be lucky if I could count my real friends on one hand. I remember thinking how absurd a statement that was as I counted off hand-after-hand with the litany of my many childhood friends.

It's funny how few of those names I remember now.

Somewhere along the path I stopped making friends so easily. I think it was about the time when I got married, had children, and settled down. Suddenly, my circle of friends wasn't my real family anymore. The circle had spun us out, one after another to the corners of the country. Now I can barely count to five.

That's why I'm so excited about my new friends. Last night I got a call from Dave. He wanted to know how the defective siding on my house was holding up. I told him that I hired two teenagers to paint over the problem. When Dave said "twice the help for half the money," I knew I'd latched onto a wise one.

My New Friends

You know how friends can be so practical when you're unsure of yourself? That's my new friend Dave all over. The guy is a rock. He wouldn't let me dwell on my siding problems. Instead, he asked me if I have any nicks or cracks on my windshield that need to be glazed over. He said this with such a hopeful tone that I was reluctant to tell him I don't have a car.

Well, now he knows. You can't hide secrets from your friends. So I blabbed it all and told him about my bad day at the office, my receding hairline, and the moles in my back yard. Dave is a guy who is accustomed to thinking that there's never been a problem that a home equity loan can't solve, so my confessions threw him off momentarily. After a long pause, Dave said he'd get back to me on the moles. I'm expecting a call on that any day now.

A lot of my new friends like used clothing, so I try to help them out when I can. We never seem to be able to get together for a cup of coffee, but they always wave when the truck comes around to pick up.

I have invited some of my new friends over for dinner, but they seem to prefer conferencing in at dinner time. And not all of them need used clothing. When new my buddy Jim called, I tried to set up a pick-up day, but all he wanted to talk about was what I think of Al Gore and George Bush. I had to admit that they have some nifty looking clothes, but I'm not banking on making friends with them.

So now when the talk turns to politics I try to change the subject, but it doesn't always work. The last time I tried that my new friend Carol tried to dump me. All the pain of lost friendships from the past started coming back to me, and I begged her not to hang up the phone. All Carol could say was: "Is your wife home, Mr. Rightgard?"

Momzilla

The question of what to do with the Halloween costumes from years past has come up again, and for once I've got an idea. We'll all take turns wearing them.

Last year my son was Godzilla. It must have been the year of the lizard because he also got a chameleon around the same time and named him Jake. The coroner's report hasn't come in yet, but I think Jake died of fright when the boys tried to feed him a spider. (Rest in peace, Jake.)

But Godzilla never dies. As long as there are mad scientists blowing up atomic bombs somewhere in the world, Godzilla and the other monsters born of nature's backlash against man's folly will be around to tear down high-voltage wires, topple skyscrapers, and stomp on cars.

My son's Godzilla costume has a long tail and a lizard helmet with rubber teeth that protrudes from your forehead. It's an outfit that presents a fearless image, as long as you pay no attention to the angelic face of your child peeping through the hole in the mask.

Unlike me, Godzilla is afraid of nothing. Scary monsters don't have to worry about running out of candy before all the goblins in the neighborhood get their due. I try to make our candy supply stretch by doling out one piece per customer. When we run out of goodies, I blow out the jack-o-lanterns on the front porch, and close the curtains to make it look like no one's home.

My son trick-or-treated without incident last year, so I judged the Godzilla costume to be a success. But things change fast in a child's battle to overcome his fears. This year my son is going to be a Pokemon trainer. Pokemon are a newer kind of monster that come on trading cards. Some of the Pokemon look like they could be distant relatives of Godzilla, but most of them are too cute to be scary.

It would take an exceptional actress to make Godzilla look cute. But my wife likes a challenge, so instead of buying another french maid costume this year, she decided to be Godzilla herself. (I'm afraid to go near the bedroom now, but at least I'm saving a few bucks.)

She auditioned the part while getting out the fall decorations to put up around the house. Things like friendly witches on brooms, black cats that look like they plugged in the toaster with one paw and stuck another one in the bathtub just to see how many lives they've got left, and perfect pumpkins with cozy smiles that couldn't scare a small lizard (sorry Jake).

I'm convinced that if it weren't for my wife, there wouldn't be any holidays at all, Halloween included. She's the one who gets us all in the holiday spirit when she puts the decorations out. Somehow they always come as a surprise, even though many of them look comfortingly familiar.

My contribution to Halloween is a VCR tape of a special hosted by Vincent Price. I got it free one year for buying a loaf of bread. It's a retrospective of the low-budget horror movies from the 50s like "The Blob" and "It Came From Outer Space." I play it every year over the protests of the rest of the family. Griping about the Vincent Price movie has become a treasured family tradition, so I'm happy to do my part.

But I'm not going to turn out the lights and hide in the living room this year when we run out of candy. Not when Momzilla can simply dance around on the front porch and smile.

State of the Onion Message

My fellow vegetables. I sit among you today humbled by the bountiful harvest we enjoyed this week. There are more vegetables in the bin at this moment than at any time in this great household's history.

We're getting into stews in record numbers, and celebrating the salad days of this administration. And all because of the policy of passive resistance that I, the onion, championed in the 95th Congress of Comestibles.

Look around this great white chamber. Have we ever been so well lit up before? Why, I can see clear through the vegetable bin to the deli meats and cheeses in the next compartment. I see milk and salad dressing, butter and biscuits, all the fixings for a fabulous meal. And at night I go to sleep to the sounds of the ice maker in the freezer section next door, churning out tiny ice cubes shaped like half moons while the people sleep.

And that's what it's all about, isn't it people? Giving back to the community. I remember my father, the Great Onion, rolling me around on his knee and telling me about the time his father made the people cry because he gave so much of himself. The story goes that they peeled him all the way back, layer by layer, until they reached the center. And what they found should make every onion, every vegetable, in this refrigerator proud. They found a cocktail onion. Giving back, people. Don't ever forget that.

Last week, when I sat among you for my weekly address, we could hardly stand the smell of each other. Apples were bruised and battered, carrots were going limp like noodles, lettuce was turning brown, and onions were staring to sprout. And the light in the refrigerator flickered on and off to a diabolical beat that we never could figure out.

We were trapped in a 12-year-old refrigerator through no fault of our own. But thanks to the easy credit policies of this administration, we were delivered from those deplorable conditions. The evil Darth Fridger was finally hauled away on a dolly, and Princess Layaway Plan was brought in. Isn't she a beaut?

This is the way it's supposed to be. Refrigerators should always be white. You all know the legend passed down from our forefathers. About the day the evil black refrigerator came to this house. Scary music played on the stereo, the ice maker wouldn't work, and relatives pulled the cheap plastic cover off the cold water dispenser twice in the first two weeks. The people put so much glue on that cover that they contaminated the environment for generations to come.

We're still paying the price for that pollution, even now in the clear, crisp air of the new refrigerator. Do you remember the left-over sour cream that got green slimy stuff all over itself? Bad air, I'm telling you. And what about that potato with eyes growing on it? It must have been a mutant. Some kind of crazy genetic freak. I'm starting to peel just thinking about it.

It was a hardscrabble life. Living with catsup spills, moldy cheese, and tuna casseroles slowly turning their plastic containers into mausoleums for wayward meals. You baby carrots take note. When you were just tiny seeds in a packet somewhere, we lived under the dominion of the evil empire.

The worst part of living in Darth Fridger was being stuck in the dark when the lights went out. You couldn't even see the vegetable sitting right next to you. Oh, the songs we used to sing to keep our spirits up in the blackened void. Little tunes like "There's Always Tomorrow" and the theme song from Star Wars. We knew that Luke and the freedom fighters would one day come to rescue us and rid the world of the evil Darth Fridger.

But it was getting harder and harder to keep hope alive. Every weekend, the man of the house would open the door and say the same thing: "There's nothing wrong with this refrigerator." Then he'd get out a can of beer with not so much as a nod to the vegetable bin. Why, he scarcely knew we even existed.

Somebody had to get his Visa card and restore order to the galaxy. And it was the princess, I'm sure. She was the only one who ever took the time to look in on us vegetables. She put the baby carrots in here, entrusting those tender young souls to our care. She kept the fruits fresh, and always had a kind word for young master Luke.

The young boy of the household showed promise right from the start. Why, he could steer clear of a square meal on pure instinct and find the treats blindfolded. The force was always strong with master Luke.

State of the Onion Message

So be of good cheer as we enter the new grocery week. The galaxy has at last entered a new epoch of light and laughter. And most of us have only got a week to enjoy it, so let's make the most of our time. God bless you fellow vegetables, and God bless the new fridge.

Computer Problems

I have to use a computer at work, so my family thinks that I know everything about them. My assignment, therefore, even before I decide to accept it, is to fix our home computer every time it breaks.

Most of the time this isn't a big problem. When things go kablooey, I usually just turn off the machine and turn it back on again. That seems to handle most situations. But the other day my wife and daughter got together and decided to really test my computer skills.

I was deep into coaching a football game halfway across the country when I got the call. "Dad. The computer's acting funny."

No problem, I thought. I'll just warm up my hands on the sideline, run upstairs, and yank the power cord out of the wall.

But something different on the computer screen this time stopped me in my tracks. There was a big message box that said: "Cannot read from drive C." I'd never seen that error message before, and I had a sneaking suspicion as I unplugged the power cord that the old drop kick in the end zone might not work this time.

The computer booted up as usual, and then said: "Cannot read from drive C." There was a cancel button there, so I tried that on the harebrained theory that I might not need any of the programs or data files on the hard disk. That made the whole screen go gunnysack.

My wife and daughter patted me on the back, and went off to find something to work on that wasn't broken. That left just me and the computer. A computer that couldn't read from drive C.

Maybe the computer just needs some reading lessons, I thought. People go back to school all the time to brush up their skills, so why shouldn't my computer?

When you think about it, our computer has been over-worked with financial records, brownie recipes, flyers for my wife's brave bunch of elementary school volunteers, and sixth-grade homework assignments on things like the egyptian pyramids and hieroglyphics.

What if our computer got too involved with the data my family has been entering and started trying to read hieroglyphics on drive C? That would certainly confuse things. As I explained to my daughter the egyptian princess, nobody could figure out what hieroglyphics meant until someone found the rosetta stone. They used that like a dictionary to look up what all the funny looking characters meant, and read the hieroglyphics that had mystified scientists for so long.

OK. I thought. Now I'm onto something. I hauled out the dictionary and started flipping the pages in front of the computer monitor like that guy on The Outer Limits who could read really fast. A light was blinking next to the hard drive, so I figured something good was happening.

I got so excited with my initial success that I decided to go beyond the basics of the language to some of the fun stuff. I got out my book of Calvin and Hobbes comics, and put a few of those up next to the screen. That made the light by the hard drive go crazy.

Things pretty much got back to normal after that, but every once in a while I'll be working on the family finances or something, and a picture of Calvin will pop up on the screen. That's my signal to stop counting pennies and read a few comics to the computer. Lifelong learning has become a way of life for us now. And we keep coming back to Calvin and Hobbes because they teach us that there's magic in the mundane when you learn to use your imagination.

My wife can't figure out how I get anything done with the computer unplugged, but I'm afraid that if I reboot now it will spoil the fun.

Kitchen Floor As History

Archaeologists have had a lot of luck lately digging up fossils and frozen animals deep in the tundra of Siberia. The technique here is simple. You just peel back layer after layer of snow and sedimentary rock until you find something interesting. The latest discovery was a 20,000-year-old woolly mammoth that somehow got stuffed into a giant ice cube. (How'd you like to find that floating around in your cocktail?)

While contemplating that possibility, I got to looking at my kitchen floor, and thought I saw a gleam of something poking through a hole in one of our vinyl tiles. I was on my hands and knees in no time clawing at the edges of the tile until I could peel it back all the way and see what was underneath there. And what I found goes right to the heart of what's wrong with America today. Yes. It was another stick-on vinyl tile. The tile was woefully out of date, almost campy in appearance, but I had to admit that it was mine because I recognized the pattern.

Exhausted after pulling up that tile, I sat back for a minute to admire my handiwork. I now had a kitchen floor that was all white with a black crisis-cross pattern, except for the one blue tile I had unearthed next to the refrigerator.

Before you know it, I was lost in sentimental memories about the blue tile. Ah, it the was early 90s when we got that floor. Things were better then, I seem to recall. I didn't worry as much about the stock market because I didn't own any stock, and I was optimistic about the future.

My curiosity piqued, I was soon back on the floor digging at that blue tile with a butter knife. I knew there was something underneath there, something from my past that would shed more light on my personal history, an artifact of semi-antiquity, possibly from an era known only as the 80s.

And there it was. Just as I suspected. Another stick-on tile. This one was green, the color of money, because the 80s were all about money, the decade of greed. Unfortunately, I had even less money in the 80s than I did in the 90s. I was beginning to see why archaeologists can't afford to wear anything but khaki shorts and sandals. They keep going back in time until they're broke.

There must have been something good about the 80s. Maybe that was the decade when they relaxed the rules on how many layers of stick-on vinyl tiles you can put down before you have to buy a real floor.

I was getting in pretty deep now, so I put up some scaffolding and grabbed a football helmet with a flashlight strapped to the top so that I could peer further into the depths of my kitchen's past.

I fought my was past cigarette burns in the orange tiles we had back in the 70s and soon found bits of pressed vegetables that never made it all the way back to the fridge. It was becoming obvious that whoever lived in my kitchen 30 years ago was a slob. Oh, yeah. That was me. Well, things weren't always better in the good-old days.

I like vegetables a lot better now, and I even clean the floor once in a while. But this depressing tile on the kitchen floor has got to go. My expedition back through my kitchen's history reminded me of how far we've come as a society, as well as the futility of simply covering up our past transgressions.

So I'm coming clean for the new millennium. Instead of a new batch of stick-on tiles on top of the heap, I'm ripping it all out. The Smithsonian may be interested in a cross-section of the old floor for posterity, but I'm throwing the rest in the dumpster and looking forward to walking on a clean slate.

Letter to Oman

Dear Ashish,

Hello, my friend! I was very happy indeed to receive your letter. Omani stamps are so lovely. I can never decide whether to steam them off and put them in my album or leave them on the envelope along with your crazy handwriting.

Did you enjoy the Love Boat tapes that I sent you? I hope the local police were not in a rough mood when they arrived. I remember too well what happened when you were caught watching reruns of Love American Style and sentenced to five years of hard labor for being in possession of a bad show.

I know that was a difficult time for you, as it was for me, knowing that I had a small part to play in your incarceration. But our friendship flourished during those years when you had nothing better to do than become my pen pal, so jail wasn't all bad.

You will be saddened to learn that John Elway has retired. I know that you idolized him for his suffering with dignity through four superbowl losses. I neglected to tell you that he finally won the superbowl twice in a row, because I feared that destroying your illusions about the beauty of failure would be more than you could stand in your current state.

I say "state" advisedly, and with the full knowledge that the authorities will be reading this letter before you get it. If you don't see an air mail stamp on the envelope showing Elvis Presley gyrating next to a half-naked female teenager, you can assume that it has been confiscated and ended up in somebody else's stamp collection.

As to your state, did you try the St. Elton John's Wort? We just discovered the medicinal power of herbs over here, and many of my melancholy friends report that the wort peps them up a bit. Some of them even start singing. It's worth a try, and I'm betting your friends will be impressed if you can remember all the words to Candle in the Wind. Be careful to stay out of the sun though, or at least wear that N.Y. Yankees cap I sent you for Christmas. This wort stuff will give you a bad sunburn and turn you into a soprano if you aren't careful.

Do you still smoke those horrible little cigarettes that smell like rotten incense? I almost got arrested when I lit one up over here. You can get away with a lot of stuff in this country, but smoking camel dung in public is not allowed. Don't send me any more of those. OK?

Has life in your part of the world been exciting these past few months? I imagine there is something unnerving about watching all those F-16s taking off from the military base across from your neighborhood at all hours of the night. I did send your little ideas along to the Pentagon about how to observe the sanctity of religious holidays and stop waking people up in the middle of the night just because our clocks are off by 12 hours, but they haven't gotten back to me yet.

My suggestion to you and your neighbors is to get out your lawn chairs and a few six packs and enjoy the show. Our jets roar with fire at night! Those devils (as you call them) are playing monopoly over in Kosovo now and they need a lot of gas. I know Mediterranean and Baltic have never paid off, even with hotels, but over here we are happy just to pass GO. So tell your friends at the oil fields to keep the black gold flowing. And try to get the price down, will you?

We have a new kind of car over here called the military assault vehicle (or MAV for short) that we like to drive. It only gets two miles to the gallon, but it is guaranteed to survive any collision with a less expensive country. So we need the gas. OK?

Your friend,
Bill

Musical Poetry

I t's not hard to get poetry published, but it's kind of expensive. That's the sad conclusion I came to after years of toiling in obscurity, wrestling with my muse, and listening to the top 40 on the radio.

During all that time, it never occurred to me that my poetry should be set to music, so I was surprised when I received a letter from a company out of New York called Poetical Melodies. The letter said some very nice things about me. That I'm a poet. That my poetry has, and I quote: "that certain something." That not every poem can become a song, but mine can.

My poem would be set to original music in the style of my choice. I could have country, soul, rock, gospel, or folk. The people at Poetical Melodies even offered to choose a style for me if I couldn't make up my mind.

I now had an answer to all my problems with rhyme schemes and other technical details that poets grapple with. I could choose rock music to drown out all the clunky words with a heavy bass. And a good drummer can lay down a beat better than iambic pentameter ever could.

Or I might go with gospel to instill a deeper meaning in my poem. There is no sense in trying to be profound using just words when you have a gospel choir waiting to sing your poem out to the heavens.

My love poems might go well with country music, especially the ones about good love gone bad. Country is good for that.

Or folk. Isn't that kind of like Bob Dylan? He wrote some good poems. I could almost do that if I had the right music.

My head was swimming with the possibilities, and my poems were jumping out of the desk drawer to stage impromptu auditions. What a pathetic sight! Poems are not supposed to make their own music. That's why we have companies like Poetical Melodies. I had several poems attempting to play classical music, even though the letter clearly stated that classical was not a choice. They seemed undaunted even after I gave them the bad news. (Classicists are like that.)

A few poems going for the soul sound made a mockery of Motown with a poorly staged rendition of "I Got You Babe." Talk about confused! I thought my poems would hold together a little better than that.

They all wanted to be on the cassette tape that Poetical Melodies offered to create for a reasonable production fee of $199.

Coming up with the 200 clams wasn't going to be too difficult. I've still got room for one more home equity line of credit. But picking out just one lucky poem from the masses in my drawer all yearning to be free, hoping to become a song, might just push me over the edge. Then nobody would get a song.

The solution was so obvious that I almost missed it. The people at Poetical Melodies are the professionals in this situation. They know all about my poetry—the letter said so. My poetry sang to them. If they could pick a music style, then they would surely have no trouble selecting the right poem to go with it. All I needed was a box big enough to hold all my poems and about 200 dollars worth of stamps.

I can't wait to get my musical poem, and I'm hoping that the poems that don't make the cut will be able to fend for themselves all right on the streets of New York. I'm going to miss those crazy kids. I thought about alerting all the Broadway producers to the prospect of a few new talents in the area, but decided to let my poems just take New York by surprise. If they can make it there, they'll make it anywhere.

The Alien Handbook

S cientists now say that life is rare in the cosmos, that the possibility of alien life forms is not nearly as inevitable as we once thought. Despite Carl Sagan's enthusiasm about the billions and billions of stars in the sky, the new theory is that human beings may be all alone in the universe.

These scientists have evidently not been to my house. I have suspicions about several members of my family. They might be aliens. There might be some at your house too.

Having battled what I think may be aliens in disguise for most of my life, I am now in a position to offer some suggestions for identifying species from other planets masquerading in our midst.

When someone who looks like your wife suddenly bursts into the garage wearing a smile like Jack Nicholson's twisted grin in The Shining, and asks you to look at the new pictures in the bathroom, be on alert.

You will most likely be forced to march into the bathroom and examine the crime scene. At this juncture, I suggest that you play it cool. Aliens can tell when you are being insincere. Pause for a few seconds to appraise the pictures, and summon up your enthusiasm for a hearty: "They look great honey! How much did they cost?"

If this is a real alien visitation and not just a figment of your imagination, the answer will definitely be: "They were on sale!"

Aliens posing as children are harder to spot, possibly because children are new to this world anyway and thus have a ready stock of excuses for what would otherwise appear to be irrational behavior.

However, after years of service as a captive audience in my own home, I have arrived at the conclusion that a child who can't stop giggling and repeats the phrase "potty head" more than 50 times in the same day is most likely not from this planet. Pictures from the Mars Rover confirmed that there are no toilets on Mars, so I think that explains the fascination that aliens seem to have with these plumbing fixtures.

Another sign that your child has been abducted and temporarily replaced by an alien in disguise is a habit of collecting pets. If your kids ask for lizards, rabbits, fish, frogs, cats, and dogs, you may be assured that they are not just for casual observation. Have you ever wondered why the light in your child's bedroom is always on at three o'clock in the morning while everyone else is asleep? Animal experiments is my guess. That would explain the mysterious death of Jake the lizard after only two weeks in his $90 terrarium, and the sudden appearance of seven baby guinea pigs in an unattended cage.

These guinea pigs seem to squeal at a frequency perfectly tuned for sending radio signals to the gamma quadrant. That's another clue right there. I now believe that guinea pigs are used by aliens like extraterrestrial cell phones to communicate with their home planet.

And what about cats? There must be an explanation for the cool, penetrating gaze of our feline friends. I'm afraid that this superior attitude is based on the knowledge that people make perfectly good servants when allowed to think that they are really in charge. I've always wondered why our cat never comes when I call his name or whistle, but in the spirit of humanity I have attributed this lack of success to some failure on my part. Aliens disguised as cats are very happy to indulge such self-defeating fantasies.

When aliens are everywhere around you, it's hard not to question yourself when you look in the mirror. I think this explains why men grow beards or mustaches, and woman change their hair styles and colors every so often. It would be awful to discover that we weren't really who we thought we were, so we keep evolving, works in progress steam rolling towards a destiny we can never know in advance.

The good news about aliens is that they have a low tolerance for boredom, and will very likely leave your home just as suddenly as they arrived. In the end, life in the suburbs isn't cosmopolitan enough for creatures who can just as easily invade some unsuspecting hosts in New York or Los Angeles. After a few weeks of Hollywood Squares and Who Wants to Be a Millionaire on TV every night after dinner, you will once again hear your wife vowing not to use the credit card again this month, the children doing their homework without giggling, and the household pets quietly settled back into their proper places. Ah, life is good when you're not an alien.

Coin of the Realm

O ne hundred dollar bills used to inspire good capitalists like myself. Whenever I saw someone whip out a hundred dollar bill in the supermarket checkout line, I was impressed, even if the person was wearing slippers and a housecoat.

There was always something about that small picture of Benjamin Franklin, perfectly centered and looking erudite and masterly, that made me feel rich with history and proud to be an American with a promising future for the next two minutes, which is the average time it takes me to spend a hundred dollars.

Again, however, the out-of-work cartoonists have found employment in a heretofore serious occupation, the engravers desk at the Federal Bureau of Money. They got a hold of Ben and enlarged his already prominent forehead to the point where a man is tempted to get out his skis and slalom down past Ben's eyebrows for a triple back flip off his nose.

Not that a hundred dollars isn't cause for celebration. It's just that Ben's head is so big now that I want to rent the space for an advertisement or give him a few aspirin and tell him he'll be all right in the morning.

As if a forehead bigger than Argentina weren't embarrassing enough, they picked Ben up and put him down left of center on the bill. And poor Ben thought he was done with politics when he signed the Declaration of Independence and went off to fly kites in the middle of thunderstorms.

The rascals at the root of this chicanery started with the one hundred dollar bill, but they didn't stop there. Next to go was Andrew Jackson. I never minded his windswept hairdo when his picture was small on the twenty dollar bill. A small flip of hair is tolerable. But when they enlarged Andrew Jackson's head and knocked him off center on the twenty, that hair started to bother me. I know that Dippity Do has been around for some time, but I never guessed that it dated back to the early 1800s. How else do you explain hair that looks like the southern approach to Mount Everest? It's not natural.

I suppose it won't be long before Thomas Jefferson gets a big head on the five dollar bill and starts thinking he's the father of half our country. George Washington may not like losing full ownership of that title, but when people get big heads all kinds of trouble usually results.

Anyone who doesn't believe Thomas Jefferson is really the father of half the country may now get out the phone book and count the number of Jeffersons in there. I want a full report on my desk in the morning.

George Washington never lied when he was small on the one dollar bill, the backbone of America. But I'm scared. What's going to happen when they make him bigger and destroy the careful symmetry and delicate balance of the dollar? I recall too well the mayhem that ensued in 1979 when Susan B. Anthony showed up on a funny looking quarter that wouldn't fit in any vending machines. Our great country was deep in recession at the time, and people took out their anger on the obvious culprit—that horrible coin. It didn't look substantial enough to be worth a dollar. This was the most direct evidence ever that rampant inflation had cut into not only our buying power, but also our national bravado.

Let's not pull George Washington's wig into a twist by blowing him up on the dollar bill just when inflation is finally under control. I didn't get much consolation in the 70s from melting down my Susan B. Anthony dollars into wind chimes (although my neighbors seem to enjoy them), and I don't want to aggravate any more founding fathers by making them big enough to reveal their flaws.

We Want The Blimp!

Most Americans are accustomed to watching sporting events where a big blimp provides pictures of the stadium from high up in the sky. The broadcasters never fail to mention the blimp, and there is usually at least one shot of the thing floating around up there. Sometimes they even show a pilot with headphones on sitting in the cockpit. The pilot usually waves and smiles like there's nothing better in this world than sitting at the controls of a blimp.

I hate to pop the balloon here, but the truth is there is no blimp. That's right. That overhead photo of a football stadium that you see on TV is actually a picture taken by a U2 spy plane back in 1958. They just keep showing the same picture over and over again. The announcers always say "Isn't that a beautiful sight?" like they've never seen it before, but that's only because they're in on the con. Before you can get a job as an announcer, you have to promise never to tell anybody that the blimp is actually a plastic toy hung from fishing line in a photography studio in Burbank with fake sky and clouds as a backdrop.

Did you ever notice how those clouds never move? My research shows that on a good day with favorable breezes a blimp can reach top speeds of about three miles per hour. So how could the blimp possibly cover a game in Miami on Sunday morning and then make another appearance in Denver for the afternoon game? And then be in San Diego in time for Monday Night Football? Please, folks. Don't make me do the math here. It just doesn't add up.

Network honchos are no dummies. They know that people go for blimps because, like balloons, blimps are whimsical creations of man's imagination, born of the universal desire to defy gravity and float in the clouds.

There was a report a few years back about a guy in Los Angeles who liked balloons so much that he tied a few hundred of them to a lawn chair and strapped himself in. They finally found him at 20,000 feet giving the thumbs-up sign to all the passengers in a 747 that was whizzing by.

The problem with blimps is that they don't look serious enough. To get anything built in this country you have to go through the Congress of the United States of America. And the people in Congress try to look serious at all costs, even when they are spending billions of dollars on B2 bombers that you can't use in the rain. Congress never orders a blimp. These people have no sense of humor. Blimps do very well in the rain, by the way, because they float.

The battle of the blimps would be a much more civilized way to fight a war. We could send them out at the first sign of tension and watch them bump into each other like floating sumo wrestlers in the sky. Since you only need one guy to fly a blimp, this would really cut down on war casualties.

We Want The Blimp!

So let's put a stop to this conspiracy right now and build a blimp. A country that can put a man on the moon ought to be able to send a real blimp to the superbowl for once. (Unless we never really got to the moon.)

China Steals American Graffiti

T he CIA was at Grumman's Chinese Theater in Los Angeles yesterday to put their feet in the concrete for good, and announce the culmination of a decade-long investigation into the theft of American movies by the Chinese government.

Industry observers and late-night television viewers alike seemed unsurprised when told that the George Lucas classic, American Graffiti, has turned up missing from the vault in Hollywood. One sloe-eyed observer commented that: "Yeah, man. That movie hasn't been on TV for years. I was starting to get suspicious."

Few details about the theft were available at press time, but this much was confirmed. A man known only as Lee Lee, a janitor who worked at several major studios, has been pirating movies from the vault for years.

Apparently, Lee never aroused suspicion because he liked cowboy and indian movies, and nobody missed them when they were gone. But when American Graffiti disappeared, people noticed.

A coalition of aging stars from American Graffiti, led by Ron Howard, has now come forward to protest this bold move by the Chinese. At a hastily called press conference, Richard Dreyfus, Cindy Williams, and Wolfman

Jack combined to lead a large contingent of baby boomers in the crowd protesting the theft of this last bit of documentary evidence that they once were young.

Howard announced that the group would form the nucleus of a special forces team, anchored by the surviving members of the American Graffiti cast, that will go over to China to retrieve this symbol of our cultural identity. Even Suzanne Sommers was persuaded to defer her busy infomercial taping schedule to join the mission. Several boxes of guy-masters were spotted in the back seat of her Thunderbird, but Sommers denied that they would be used on the mission, citing international laws against cruel and unusual punishments.

Experts familiar with insiders known to the group confirmed that Harrison Ford would be leading the quest, and had already been spotted in Studio B looking around for his bull whip.

In a related quirk resulting from over-participation in popular culture, Andy Griffith showed up at the press conference and told Opie that he wasn't going anywhere but back to bed. He was soon quieted by the crowd, but vowed to come back as Ben Matlock and get to the bottom of the problem using nothing but southern charm.

Foreign correspondents now believe that American Graffiti has been hidden high up in the Himalayas, near Tibet, possibly in Shangri-la. The assault force seemed a little out of shape for mountain climbing, but Richard Gere promised to call the Dalai Lama and get some good vibes going for the group. And Wolfman Jack was already yodeling up a storm in anticipation of jammed radio transmissions at the higher elevations. The call of the wild was once again validated when several hundred stray dogs showed up at the press conference and growled at reporters.

George Lucas will, of course, be directing the mission from his studio in Northern California, using advanced special effects technology. Sources say that a huge battle station camouflaged to look like Mel's Drive-In will be deployed in continuous orbit over China to distract the Chinese public with cheeseburgers and cherry cokes while the U.S. special forces team goes in to get our movie back.

Government officials expressed confidence in the special forces team, and even winked at Suzanne Sommers. But privately, many feared that when we do get American Graffiti back, the credits will be altered to say Made in China, and the international version will turn out to be a bomb.

Letter of Complaint

D ear Mr. Woods:
Oak Forever stinks. After spending $2,000 dollars at your store, I expected to get something better than a Christmas card with bits of moldy straw stuffed into the envelope in return. I can get Christmas cards that don't smell from my family. All I want from Oak Forever is a new chair.

The kitchen set I bought from you clowns now has three matching oak chairs and a small stool left over from one of the children's play sets. Obviously an emergency situation. The missing chair snapped like a twig when a light breeze came thought the window and tipped my son over while he was leaning back on it. As I explained to you earlier, my son is a budding gymnast and might very well be the next Bela Canoli, or whoever that fantastic guy from Romania was, so I can't very well blame the broken chair on him.

Since my chair was under the fabulous forever warranty, Oak Forever promised to replace it. In fact, my first impression was excellent, as my situation was handled by a man named Ken Woods (serial number 436-75). He was quick to temporarily replace the broken chair with a loner from your store and promised to order a brand new matching chair from the warehouse for me.

Unfortunately, the loner chair that was supposed to be a temporary favor to us has become the source of a nightly dispute with my family. Nobody wants to sit on it because of the whoopee cushion bolted to the seat. I suppose Ken thinks this is funny.

I realized that getting a replacement chair would take time. The receptionist (Anne Woods, serial number 436-78) even called to reassure me that the order would be followed up promptly. Again, I felt for a moment that your outfit stood for a quality product and good service.

But another month elapsed without any wood from Oak Forever. At that point, I obtained the manager's vital information (Glenn Woods, serial number 436-77). Glenn informed me that nothing had been done on my order. I told Glenn that I felt I was getting the runaround, and he assured me that he would call the warehouse and take care of things. He then proceeded to ride circles around me on a small tricycle while standing on one hand and honking an obnoxious horn. He finally calmed down when I told him about the whoopee cushion on our temporary chair. Glenn said he would talk to Ken about that. Again, all seemed well.

Another two weeks passed with no word on the status of my chair. At a dinner party, one of my husbands's business associates had the misfortune of sitting in the loner chair. This fellow claimed that he had never heard of whoopee cushions, and tried to bluff his way past the noises throughout dinner, much to the astonishment of the rest of our guests. Did a man named Robert Woods (serial number 436-79) ever work at Oak Forever?

Letter of Complaint

It has now been four months since I was told that I would get a brand-new matching chair for my kitchen under the Oak Forever warranty program. But every time I talk to you clowns, I get the warehouse line. "It's at the warehouse. I'll call the warehouse. Better check with the warehouse." Where is this warehouse that your employees keep talking about? I sincerely hope you are not still running Oak Forever out of that big tent in the municipal park, because that would be a code violation.

 I realize now why you give away cotton candy and a free pull on the Emperor Zora Tells Your Fortune machine with every purchase. It's because of your lack of good furniture. And don't think those clowns that you call employees are going to fool me anymore. I will never again duck under the flaps of Oak Forever, and I'm telling all my friends about the chair with the whoopee cushion. And you can take me off your Christmas card list. OK?

Two Socks, One World

S ocks are leading indicators of cosmic matters. Anyone who has ever dragged their dirty clothes to the laundromat and dragged back a similar but alarmingly different set of garments can tell you that. What is perhaps less apparent is that putting on the wrong socks can lead to all manner of trouble that most people are not aware of. I know because I recently took an expedition in suburbia with two different socks on. I escaped with my life, thankfully, after a harrowing adventure, and am now in a position to share my story with the outside world (places other than suburbia).

It all started one day in the fall. It was late fall, so the days had begun to shorten, which required me to rise from bed before sunrise (an unnatural by-product of the industrial revolution, this getting up before the sun). In my haste to get properly dressed for a fresh new day battling corruption and fouling up bad guys, I opened my sock drawer in the dark and pulled out a couple of good candidates for the shoes I had in mind for that particular day.

The socks went on neatly enough, but to be honest, I wasn't paying proper attention to the task at hand. If I was, I would have noticed that one sock was green and the other white. (All socks tend to look the same in the dark.) The matter of two different socks posed little trouble for me during my morning rituals. It was only later, when I ventured out of doors on my way to work that I began to see the difficulty of going out into the world with two different socks on, a green one and a white, to be exact.

My neighbor was out retrieving his morning newspaper from the puddle on his driveway, and stopped me in my tracks with a disapproving glare. "You have two different socks on" says he, as he wrings the water out of the paper. I quickly confirmed this observation, and decided it was better to get to work on time wearing two different socks than it was to stroll in late dressed correctly. That was my second mistake, but I'm getting ahead of myself.

Walking with two different socks on is not too difficult, but it can be amusing to innocent bystanders. The trick is to synchronize the gallant, vibrant steps of the foot in the green sock with the milk-toast, scaredy-cat steps of the foot in the white sock. For those of you unfamiliar with genetics, white socks have been bred to be ashamed of themselves due to years of ridicule in high schools all across this great land of ours. This is what accounts for their shy behavior in public, even when worn properly with sneakers. Do not attempt to wear white socks with black shoes unless you are planning a career as a rodeo clown. They buck like mad. Green socks are a strong breed. They are brimming with confidence, and have little tolerance for the less-than-mighty.

I staggered down the street in my neighborhood amid a chorus of hecklers, all of whom were only too glad to start their day with a good laugh at my expense. Now and then my green sock took offense and kicked a snarling dog or two with a glancing blow that could easily be excused as a simple mis-step. The owners of these vicious beasts elected to withdraw rather than challenge a man wearing two different socks. A wise decision as it turns out.

Safely out of the neighborhood, I proceeded to stop traffic for two miles on the highway when I dove into the crosswalk of the four-lane thoroughfare just as the light was beginning to turn. I can thank my green sock for that bit of recklessness. My white sock had a stroke right on the spot, and was unable to continue. This caused me to stretch in ways that Jack Lalane never recommended, and reduced my perspective to a looking-up sort of view which makes studded monster truck tires appear even more menacing than they already are.

I fought the urge to become two different people right on the spot and let the socks win. Somehow, I scraped and pulled my body through the intersection, and leapt to my feet on the other side of the highway. My green sock was so happy to have run the gauntlet successfully that it broke into an Irish jig. My white sock was shocked to see this cavalier attitude about our narrow escape, and tried to hide behind the traffic signal. Sirens ensued, and official representatives of the establishment soon arrived to help me out of my predicament.

After the attending policeman had finished their retrospective demonstration on medieval torture, and my joints snapped back into place, I resumed my pilgrimage to work. The rush hour traffic had eased at this point, so my side-kicks into oncoming traffic only hit a few cars.

When I finally reached my place of employment it was well past noon. This required an explanation. And as luck would have it, my green sock did all the talking.

Fuzzy Math

When I was in high school, one of the popular bits of sophomoric wisdom was that you would never need to know algebra in the real world. That variables and equations had no bearing on real life. And yet, despite my misgivings about its relevance, I made it through algebra all right thinking all the while that it was actually a kind of punishment inflicted by adults on young people as an antidote to youthful exuberance.

Now that I'm a certified adult, I can say from experience that I went for more than 30 years without once balancing an equation. In that time, my exuberance level has been sustained by the knowledge that a lot of things in life are not deterministic, that the approximate explanation is sometimes the best fit.

But then came the ultimate pop quiz in the form of a teenage daughter with a question about her homework.

So they were right. One does, after all, need to know algebra.

My daughter had been given a sticky homework problem in "pre-algebra," which is a euphemistic term along the lines of "slightly pregnant" as near as I can tell. Once you put your X and Y together there's no going back until you've got an equation or a baby. The question seemed deceptively simple, but proved to be difficult to solve.

We worked on the math problem together until my daughter had carefully bitten her nails down several millimeters, and I had thinned out the old growth forest on my head to keep it from catching on fire. But this was one math problem that simply would not yield to the scientific method.

After dinner, while the rest of the family retired to their leisurely pursuits, I remained at the kitchen table with my worksheets and pencils, determined to get it right. I diagrammed and charted, and stared at the kitchen ceiling for inspiration. I even took a side road to geometry for a while (not recommended).

I finally had met my match, and I never saw it coming, unless it was in the hopeful face of a loving daughter steadfastly fixed on the idealistic notion that dad was the only infallible thing in the world, the one constant star.

Late into the night, as I continued my epic struggle, delirium set in. I imagined that my own math teacher had come back, like the ghost of algebra past, to spur me on. "Apply yourself," I could almost hear him say.

But my mind wandered. I thought about all the competent parents tucking their children into bed in plenty of time to watch David Letterman, and wished I was smart enough to join them. I imagined how great it would feel to finally solve the impossible math problem. And I pressed on.

The next morning, I scraped myself off the kitchen table like a deflated party balloon, and dragged myself to work, lamenting my failure.

But when I got home that night, my daughter was in a fabulous mood. To my surprise, she discovered that the math problem was just a "challenge" question. The teacher didn't expect anyone to actually solve it, since that would require a full head of hair (see Einstein) and a high school diploma (one for two doesn't count).

It took me a few days to recover from the incident, but in that split-second when my daughter told me that the math problem was nearly, but not quite impossible, I breathed a sigh of relief. I had very nearly gotten it right, and sometimes exuberance without exactness just has to be good enough.

Quick Order Form

Whimsy Street makes a great gift! Why not order a copy today for a friend or family member? Just send a check for $13.95 (includes shipping and handling) for each book to:

Deutsa Power Press
P.O. Box 5818
Beaverton, OR 97006-0818

Your Name & Address:
Name: _____
Address: _____
City: _____ State:_____ Zip:_____

Destination Name & Address:
Name: _____
Address: _____
City: _____ State:_____ Zip:_____

Note: Only available in the United States of America.

Quick Order Form

Whimsy Street makes a great gift! Why not order a copy today for a friend or family member? Just send a check for $13.95 (includes shipping and handling) for each book to:

Deutsa Power Press
P.O. Box 5818
Beaverton, OR 97006-0818

Your Name & Address:
Name: _____
Address: _____
City: _____ State:_____ Zip:_____

Destination Name & Address:
Name: _____
Address: _____
City: _____ State:_____ Zip:_____

Note: Only available in the United States of America.

Quick Order Form

Whimsy Street makes a great gift! Why not order a copy today for a friend or family member? Just send a check for $13.95 (includes shipping and handling) for each book to:

Deutsa Power Press
P.O. Box 5818
Beaverton, OR 97006-0818

Your Name & Address:
Name: _____
Address: _____
City: _____ State:_____ Zip:_____

Destination Name & Address:
Name: _____
Address: _____
City: _____ State:_____ Zip:_____

Note: Only available in the United States of America.